PET Result

Workbook with key

Jenny Quintana

OXFORD
UNIVERSITY PRESS

Great Clarendon Street, Oxford OX2 6DP

Oxford University Press is a department of the University of Oxford.
It furthers the University's objective of excellence in research, scholarship,
and education by publishing worldwide in

Oxford New York

Auckland Cape Town Dar es Salaam Hong Kong Karachi
Kuala Lumpur Madrid Melbourne Mexico City Nairobi
New Delhi Shanghai Taipei Toronto

With offices in

Argentina Austria Brazil Chile Czech Republic France Greece
Guatemala Hungary Italy Japan Poland Portugal Singapore
South Korea Switzerland Thailand Turkey Ukraine Vietnam

OXFORD and OXFORD ENGLISH are registered trade marks of
Oxford University Press in the UK and in certain other countries

ISBN: 978 0 19 481717 2

Printed in China

This book is printed on paper from certified and well-managed sources.

ACKNOWLEDGEMENTS

The publisher would like to thank the following for permission to reproduce photographs:
Adrian Gray p.25 (Balancing Stones); Alamy pp.7 (Airline boarding pass/
Nick Gregory), 9 (young man/Big Cheese Photo LLC), 29 (bucket/Jan Tadeusz),
29 (frying pan/Caro), 29 (lamp/Nikreates), 29 (corkscrew/PhotoSpin, Inc),
29 (rubbish bin/D. Hurst), 35 (students/PhotoAlto); Corbis UK Ltd. pp.15
(Philippe Petit/Lan), 20 (Lewis Hamilton/Andy Rain/Epa), 29 (iron/Lawrence
Manning), 29 (mug/Kristy-Anne Glubish/Design Pics), 32 (Anousheh Ansari/
Sergei Ilnitsky/Epa), 48 (lie detector/Colin Anderson/Brand X); kimages.com
p.29 (tea towel/Will Heap); Elyce Feliz p.23 (Pyramid Hill Sculpture Park &
Museum); Getty Images pp.38 (woman/Image Source), 38 (couple/Leon/Riser),
40 (Amazon reflection/Photographer's Choice/Marcus Lyon), 47 (graffiti artist/
Mark Ralston/AFP); Oxford University Press pp.6 (zebra skin), 9 (brunette
girl) 9 (blonde girl/Photodisc), 29 (fan/Photodisc), 29 (vase/Stockbyte), 38
(businessman/Image Source); Photolibrary Group p.45 (DJ/Len Rubenstein/
Index Stock Imagery); Press Association Images p.15 (Philippe Petit walking
between the World Trade Centre Towers, NYC/Associated Press); Royal
Geographical Society p.39 (rubbish on Everest/Roger Mear); Superstock Ltd.
p.22 (houseboats in Seattle)

Illustrations by: Julia Barber p.7; Otto Detmeer p.50; Jessie Ford/CIA Illustration
p.44; Joy Gosney pp.14, 30; Peter Mac pp.10, 11, 12, 16, 24, 28, 37, 49;
MagicTorch pp.17, 34; Glen McBeth pp.19, 35; Josh McKible pp.8, 36, 38, 46
(plane); Neil Webb/Debut Art pp.13, 21, 42, 43, 46 (queue)

Pages 52–54 reproduced with the permission of Cambridge ESOL

Contents

Exam Overview

Paper 1 Reading and Writing (1 hour 30 minutes)

Reading

Part	Task type	What does it test?	Marks	What do you do?
1	Three-option multiple choice	Your ability to understand short texts	5	Read and choose one option
2	Matching	Your ability to understand longer texts	5	Match descriptions of people with short texts
3	True/False	Your ability to find specific information	10	Answer true/false questions
4	Four-option multiple choice	Your ability to understand attitude, opinion and purpose in a text	5	Answer multiple-choice questions on a longer text
5	Four-option multiple choice cloze	Your knowledge of vocabulary and grammar	10	Choose the correct options to complete a short passage

Writing

Part	Task type	What does it test?	Marks	What do you do?
1	Sentence transformations	Your knowledge of grammar	5	Change the sentence using one to three words
2	Short message	Your ability to write a short message	5	Write a short message of about 35–45 words
3	Longer piece of writing	Your accuracy and range in writing	15	Write a story or letter of about 100 words

Paper 2 Listening (about 30 minutes)

Part	Task type	What does it test?	Marks	What do you do?
1	Multiple choice	Your ability to understand short conversations	7	Listen and choose one of three pictures
2	Multiple choice	Your ability to identify detailed information in a monologue or interview	6	Choose the correct option while listening to a longer monologue or interview
3	Gap-fill	Your ability to find information in a longer monologue	6	Complete notes while listening
4	True/False	Your ability to understand detailed meaning, as well as attitude and opinions	6	Decide whether sentences are correct or incorrect

Paper 3 Speaking (10–12 minutes per pair of candidates)

Part	Task type	What does it test?	Time	What do you do?
1	Conversation between the examiner and each candidate	Your ability to talk about yourself	2–3 mins	Answer the examiner's questions
2	Candidates interact with each other in a shared task	Your ability to use functional language such as making suggestions	2–3 mins	Speak with each other using a picture for ideas
3	Individual long turn	Your ability to talk alone for one minute	3 mins	Talk about a photograph
4	Discussion between candidates	Your ability to take part in a discussion	3 mins	Discuss a topic related to Part 3

South Africa: City and Safari

South Africa is a beautiful country with a varied landscape. There are superb mountain ranges, incredible forested sea-shores, desert plains, and national parks full of amazing wild animals.
5 For the perfect holiday, try spending a few days in the city followed by a safari.

Cape Town

Cape Town is a wonderful city that offers white, sandy beaches, an exciting city centre, excellent food and great street entertainment. Take a guided tour to find
10 the best places to go. For the more adventurous, talk to the local people and find out what Cape Town's really like, or visit the fishing villages outside the city. The most memorable thing about Cape Town is its greatest natural landmark, Table Mountain, which
15 rises to 1,086m at its highest point. Try walking to the top and looking down at the city itself. If it's too far for you to walk, you can go most of the way by cable car and then walk for about another hour to the top.

Kruger National Park

After the city, it's worth heading out to the
20 countryside. There are many national parks in South Africa and there's so much to see and do in them that it's best to concentrate on visiting just one. You can always choose a different park next time you come. Kruger National Park is one of the most
25 popular places to go. You can hire a car and drive there yourself, as generally the roads are good and there are road maps available. The tourist roads in the park are also in good condition. However, if you prefer, you can join an organised safari. These can
30 last one day, or longer if you want to stay in one of the hotels or lodges in the park. Whatever your choice, look out for elephants, lions, rhinos and leopards, and for hippos bathing in the rivers and animals drinking from the muddy waterholes. Afterwards, you can carry
35 on exploring the countryside or perhaps try South Africa's biggest city, Johannesburg, which is just a few hours' drive away. Whatever part of South Africa you visit, your memories will last forever.

Reading Part 3

Read the text about South Africa, then decide if each sentence (1–6) is correct or incorrect.

1 It's a good idea to combine a city break with a country break.
2 There is little to do close to Cape Town.
3 You can travel by cable car right to the top of Table Mountain.
4 To get the most out of the countryside, it's necessary to go to several parks.
5 It's better to avoid using the roads around Kruger National Park.
6 You can stay overnight in Kruger National Park.

Vocabulary
Transport

Write the answers using the words below.

helicopter	ferry	hot-air balloon
lorry	motorbike	bicycle
underground train	boat	horse
ship	hovercraft	elephant	camel

a two forms of transport that travel in the air
....

b three animals used as forms of transport
....

c four forms of transport that travel across water
....
....

d two forms of road transport with two wheels
....

e a form of road transport with many wheels
....

f a form of transport that travels on rails
....

Grammar
The past simple and past continuous

1 Tick the correct sentences. Rewrite the incorrect sentences using the past simple or past continuous.

   a I was leaving the house at 8 o'clock this morning.

   b The boys were playing football all day.

   c I walked down the road when I met my neighbour.

   d My parents waited for me when my train arrived.

   e What were you doing when the rain started?

   f We were driving to France when the accident was happening.

2 Read the text. Then complete 1–10 with the past simple or past continuous form of the verbs in brackets.

Slow Travel

I recently (1)................(take) an unusual trip around the world with my best friend. For twelve months, we (2)................(not get) on a plane or a helicopter once. We (3)................(explore) 30 countries on six continents and (4)................(go) by camel, bike, boat, bus and train. While we (5)................(be) away, we met all kinds of interesting people. For example, while we (6)................(travel) on the Trans-Siberian Express from Moscow to Irkutsk, we (7)................(make) friends with some fishermen from Finland. Another great thing about our slow trip was that we (8)................(have) the time to learn new skills. For instance, while we (9)................(sail) from Singapore to Australia on a ten-day boat trip, some Mexican back-packers (10)................(teach) us Spanish. It really was the most interesting trip we'd ever taken.

Vocabulary
At the airport

1 Read the definitions then rearrange the letters to find the words. Check your answers in a dictionary.

   a someone travelling on a plane
      s s r e p a n e g   p.................

   b the card you show to get on a plane
      a r d n g b i o   b................. pass

   c the airport building where journeys begin and end
      a t r e m l n i   t.................

   d the place where your luggage is checked for illegal goods
      t o s c m u s   c.................

   e bags, suitcases, etc.
      g g e a b g a   b.................

   f the person who flies an aircraft
      o p t i l   p.................

   g the document that you show to enter or leave a country
      s a s p p r t o   p.................

2 Use the verbs to complete the airport procedure.

listen	check in	arrive
board	collect	go wait

   a .... at the terminal
   b .... at the desk
   c .... your boarding pass
   d .... through passport control
   e .... to the announcements
   f .... at the correct gate
   g .... your plane

Grammar
Question words

Complete the dialogues with the correct question words.

a '.................... did you go on holiday last year?'
'I went to Greece.'

b '.................... did you go to the party with last night?'
'Max and Joe.'

c '.................... did you travel to school this morning?'
'By car.'

d '.................... did you do last weekend?'
'I stayed at home.'

e '.................... much money did you spend on your shopping trip?'
'Nothing! I didn't buy anything.'

f '.................... were you late for school this morning?'
'I missed my bus.'

g '.................... did you last visit your grandparents?'
'Last weekend.'

h '.................... was your trip to Venice like?'
'It was fantastic!'

Articles

Complete the sentences with *a*, *an*, *the* or – .

a .... health and happiness are more important than money.

b A man and a woman were at the airport. .... woman was carrying a red suitcase.

c We went to .... island in the Caribbean.

d My cousin lives in .... Australia.

e .... moon shone brightly in the sky.

f .... Lake Geneva is in Switzerland.

g While we were on holiday, we met .... family from Finland.

h .... Alps are a mountain range in Europe.

i She doesn't like .... ice cream.

j .... Seine is a long river in France.

k It's raining! Can I borrow .... umbrella?

Writing Part 3

1   Read the task and paragraphs A–D. Decide which paragraph does not belong to the story and put the others into the correct order.

Your English teacher has asked you to write a story. Your story must have the following title:

A terrible holiday

Write about 100 words.

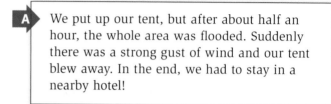

A We put up our tent, but after about half an hour, the whole area was flooded. Suddenly there was a strong gust of wind and our tent blew away. In the end, we had to stay in a nearby hotel!

B Eventually, we walked to a nearby shop and called the police. It wasn't long before they arrived and we were able to tell them what had happened.

C As we got closer to the sea, the weather began to change. At first it was a bit cloudy and rainy, but then it began to rain very hard and just as we arrived at the campsite we saw a flash of lightning.

D Last month, I went on a camping trip to the beach with some friends. We borrowed my parents' car and left early on a bright and sunny Saturday morning.

2   Write your own answer to the task in exercise 1.

2 Learning

Reading Part 2

The people in 1–3 each want to buy a book. Read the descriptions and texts A–E and decide which book is the most suitable for each person.

1   Elsa is studying French and Spanish at university and wants to read about their history. She's also keen on finding out about world issues.

2   Josie is planning to do a business course at college and would like to do some background reading before she starts. She's particularly interested in how modern world economics has developed.

3   Marc is an active person who likes travelling and is keen on nature. He's taken a couple of courses on nature and wants to read more about it.

New Beginnings

This book explores one of history's biggest economic transformations of the past 100 years. The writer explains what's really happening in Asia today, and looks at how people are making money, from selling goods in the streets to creating big finance companies.

Guide to Europe

Read about the best and most economical places to stay in Europe and which ones to avoid. Find out the best ways to discover the history and culture of each country you visit and where the best places to eat are. A must-read for anyone interested in travelling.

Lost Cultures

There are thousands of known languages in the world and around half are in danger of disappearing. In fact, many have already been lost. This book looks at why some modern languages are more popular than others and how disappearing languages affect people and their culture. A fascinating read for anyone interested in the subject.

A Language in Three Months

All the books in this series are inexpensive and easy to use with logical, clear exercises and full reference lists at the back. Books come with accompanying CD and suggestions for further online practice. Choose from a wide range of languages from Spanish to Japanese.

A Bright World

Full of beautiful illustrations and tips on how to identify wild flowers in mountainous areas, from the French Alps to the Himalayas. The author talks about the history of plants, saying why they are endangered and how conservationists are working to save them. An invaluable guide for anybody to take with them on a countryside holiday.

Grammar
Adverbs of frequency

Rewrite the sentences making sure the adverbs of frequency are in the correct place.

a ever for am I late hardly school.

b Fridays French we study on always.

c each test our gives a teacher us usually week.

d regularly until sister my midnight studies.

e bored are in these class children often.

f an have I in got never 100% exam.

Vocabulary
make, do, have, take

Choose the verb, A, B or C, which goes with the words and phrases in 1–6. Check your answers in a dictionary.

1 .... an exercise
   A make   B do   C get
2 .... a good time
   A get   B take   C have
3 .... a long time
   A take   B make   C get
4 .... a tablet
   A make   B do   C take
5 .... up your mind
   A give   B make   C get
6 .... the washing-up
   A do   B make   C have

Listening Part 4

▶1 You will hear a conversation between a girl, Sara, and a boy, Joseph, about studying for exams. Decide if each sentence is correct or incorrect.

1 At first, Joseph thinks Sara is doing enough revision.
2 Sara agrees that she needs to work harder.
3 Joseph usually studies in the mornings and in the evenings.
4 Sara is keen on having a party at her home.
5 They agree to have the party on the day after the exams.

Grammar

The present simple and present continuous

Read the text about The Palace School. Then complete 1–10 with the present simple or present continuous form of the verbs.

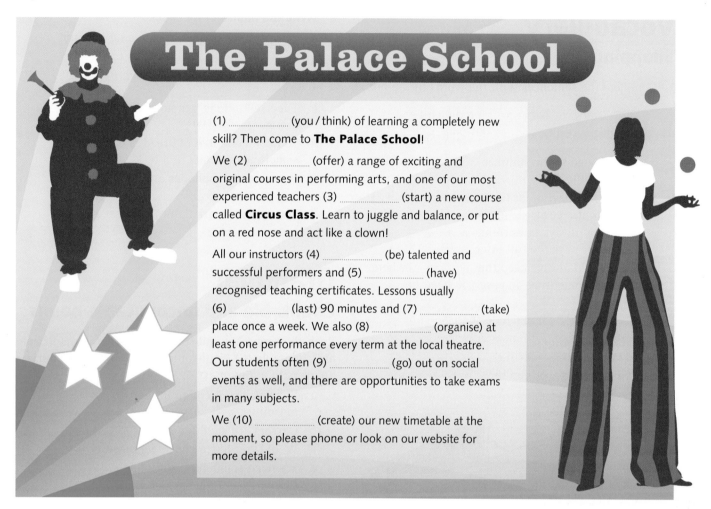

The Palace School

(1) .... (you / think) of learning a completely new skill? Then come to **The Palace School**!

We (2) .... (offer) a range of exciting and original courses in performing arts, and one of our most experienced teachers (3) .... (start) a new course called **Circus Class**. Learn to juggle and balance, or put on a red nose and act like a clown!

All our instructors (4) .... (be) talented and successful performers and (5) .... (have) recognised teaching certificates. Lessons usually (6) .... (last) 90 minutes and (7) .... (take) place once a week. We also (8) .... (organise) at least one performance every term at the local theatre. Our students often (9) .... (go) out on social events as well, and there are opportunities to take exams in many subjects.

We (10) .... (create) our new timetable at the moment, so please phone or look on our website for more details.

Writing Part 2

You have recently started a new hobby. Write an email to your English friend, Tim. In your email you should

➡ tell him what your new hobby is

➡ say why you enjoy it

➡ suggest a time and a place to meet

Write 35–45 words.

3 ▶ Buying and selling

Vocabulary
Shopping

1 Complete the sentences with the words in the box.

> cost   sales   bargain   credit card
> discount   receipt

a I usually go to the summer _____ to buy cheap clothes.

b I don't like paying for things by _____ . I prefer to use cash.

c My sister always buys things at a _____ . She never pays the full price.

d You should always keep the _____ when you buy something, in case you need to return it.

e 'Excuse me. How much do these jeans _____ ?'

f These sunglasses were a _____ . They were half their usual price.

2 Write the names of the shops.

a You can buy shampoo, medicine and sun cream in a p _____ .

b You can buy a dishwasher, an iron and a TV in an e _____ s _____ .

c They sell onions, potatoes and carrots in a g _____ .

d You can get a loaf of bread, a cake and sometimes biscuits in a b _____ .

e Trumpets, saxophones and violins are sold in a m _____ s _____ .

f You can buy pork, lamb and beef at a b _____ .

Grammar
Countable and uncountable nouns

Read the sentences and say whether the nouns in bold are countable (C) or uncountable (UC). Check your answers in a dictionary.

a I always drink **coffee** in the mornings. _____

b **Carrots** are good for you. _____

c Would you like a chocolate **biscuit**? _____

d We need some more **shampoo**. _____

e Can you get a **newspaper** while you're out? _____

f My favourite meat is **lamb**. _____

g Which do you prefer: white or brown **bread**? _____

h I spent all my **money** yesterday. _____

i She eats an **apple** every day. _____

j Where is my **hat**? _____

Reading Part 1

Read each notice 1–4 and choose A, B or C.

1

STAFF:
*Please show your discount
card before you give your
goods to the cashier.*

A Staff can pay less for their shopping.
B Staff only get a discount on some goods.
C Staff discounts are unavailable here.

2

WE ARE MOVING!
Our new clothes store
opens in George Street
on 15th July.

A The shop is closing down permanently.
B The shop is going to a new location.
C The shop is opening here in July.

3

NO REFUNDS
GIVEN WITHOUT
A RECEIPT

A This place never gives people their money back.
B This place will sometimes give refunds.
C This place only gives receipts for some items.

4

All lost car park
tickets will result
in a £20 fee.

A It always costs £20 to park here.
B You will be fined £20 if you park here.
C You must pay £20 if you have no ticket.

Grammar
Quantity

1 Underline the words or phrases of quantity in a–i.
Tick the correct sentences and correct the wrong
ones. There may be more than one possible answer.
   a I've got any great new DVDs.
   b I haven't got much clothes!
   c Would you like a few sugar in your tea?
   d How many money did you spend at the shops?
   e There are several good shops in our town.
   f I got a few CDs for my birthday.
   g Are there much chocolates left?
   h There are plenty of sandwiches if you want one.
   i How much people are coming to the party?

2 Choose the correct words to complete 1–9 in
the conversation.

Josh We need to go shopping for our party.
Anna OK. Let's write a list. Do we need
(1) *several / some / many* bread for
sandwiches?
Josh Yes, definitely. We haven't got
(2) *any / some / little* bread and we've
only got a (3) *lot / few / little* butter.
Anna What about cheese?
Josh We've got (4) *much / a lot of / a few* cheese.
Anna How (5) *much / many / few* packets
of biscuits have we got?
Josh We've got (6) *several / much / many*
packets of biscuits, but we've only
got (7) *a few / some / little* olives and we
haven't got (8) *a lot / much / many* of crisps.
Anna Right. We'll get all those and
(9) *some / much / any* drinks.

Vocabulary
Clothes and accessories

1 Write the names of the items of clothing.

1 ....
2 ....
3 ....
4 ....
5 ....
6 ....
7 ....
8 ....
9 ....
10 ....
11 ....
12 ....
13 ....

2 Choose the correct word, A, B or C, to complete the sentences. Check your answers in a dictionary.

1 You should always try .... clothes before you buy them.
   A out   B on   C up

2 My shoes are completely worn .... I must buy some new ones.
   A off   B out   C with

3 What do you prefer to ....: jeans or a skirt?
   A wear   B carry   C dress

4 Please, ... off your jacket and sit down.
   A have   B put   C take

5 What time do you usually .... dressed in the morning?
   A get   B make   C put

Writing   Part 3

1 Read part of this letter from Marco. Then read Wen's reply and correct the mistakes with punctuation.

> I've just started doing a class in English. I've met some great people and I've learned a lot.
>
> In your next letter, please tell me about your experience of learning English. What classes do you do? Do you enjoy them?

> dear marco
>
> thanks for your letter it was great to hear from you you asked me to tell you about my experience of learning english well at the moment im doing an english course at a language school and i have lessons twice a week we've got an american teacher and she's really nice
>
> last summer i did a course at a language school in london i really enjoyed being there and i met lots of really interesting people how are your family hope to hear from you soon
>
> wen

2 Write your own letter replying to Marco. Write about 100 words.

Review 1 Units 1–3

1 Read the text below and for 1–10 choose the correct answer, A, B, C or D.

Megamalls

Although Internet shopping (1)............... more and more popular, you can't beat the real thing. People love meeting their friends, going to shops, (2)............... clothes and looking for (3)................ . There are all kinds of different places to go shopping, but (4)............... people like to go to shopping centres where everything is in one place. The first shopping centre (5)............... in the US in 1922 and then, in the 1980s, giant megamalls appeared. The West Edmonton Mall in Canada had more than 800 shops, a hotel, (6)............... amusement park, a miniature-golf course, a zoo and a 134-metre-long lake. Today, the Golden Resources Shopping Mall in Beijing is the largest shopping centre in (7)............... world. It (8)............... around 1,000 shops, hundreds of restaurants, children's playgrounds and a skating rink, and it (9)............... at least two days to explore. So (10)............... can you buy there? The answer is 'almost anything'!

1 A to become   B is becoming   C becomes   D become
2 A getting up   B taking off   C wearing out   D trying on
3 A bargains   B receipts   C costs   D credits
4 A much   B lot   C plenty   D many
5 A was opening   B opened   C had opened   D has opened
6 A an   B a   C several   D little
7 A a   B any   C the   D some
8 A is having   B has   C has had   D have
9 A makes   B does   C has   D takes
10 A how   B where   C what   D when

2 For a–l choose the correct answer to complete the sentences.

a We met some interesting people when we *travelled/were travelling* around Europe.
b Our English teacher *visited/was visiting* Spain last summer.
c *How/What* do you usually get to work?
d While we were in Switzerland, we went climbing in *an/the* Alps.
e I *never am/am never* bored at weekends.
f We often *go/are going* on holiday in August.
g Did you *make/have* a good time in Italy?
h I *think/am thinking* of working in South America for six months.
i I work in a shop so I get a *discount/bargain* on what I buy.
j I don't usually try *on/out* clothes in shops.
k Can you help me *make/do* this exercise?
l My sister hardly *never/ever* pays by credit card.

3 Decide which is the odd one out in each group a–h and explain why.

a terminal   customs   ferry   boarding pass
b lorry   bicycle   hovercraft   train
c receipt   butcher's   baker's   supermarket
d sandal   belt   trainer   boot
e sugar   butter   hat   shampoo
f elephant   lamb   pork   beef
g necklace   scarf   bracelet   earring
h a few   much   several   many

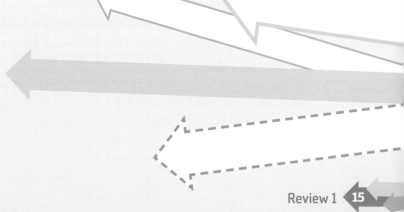

Reading Part 4

Read the text about an amazing stuntman. For questions 1–3 choose the correct answer A, B, C or D.

PHILIPPE PETIT
HIGH WIRE WALKER

On August 7, 1974, a 24-year-old French high-wire-walker called Philippe Petit performed one of the most amazing stunts the world has seen. He positioned a
5 thin cable between the former twin towers of the World Trade Centre more than 400 metres above the ground. Then he walked across the wire from building to building, doing various acrobatic movements on the way.

10 Petit performed for around an hour while an amazed crowd watched from below. When he finally came down, he was immediately arrested. The next day, his stunt made headlines and pushed major political stories off the front
15 page. He had so much publicity that in the end the charges were dropped. His stunt became known as 'the artistic crime of the century'.

Petit first became interested in performing when he was a child, after somebody gave
20 him a magic kit. He started by doing magic shows in salons around Paris. In the late 1960s, he was also one of the earliest modern-day street jugglers. He had taught himself to walk the high wire at the age of 16 and he made
25 his first illegal wire-walk in 1971, when he walked between the towers of Notre Dame Cathedral in Paris.

As well as New York and Paris, Petit has done wire-walks all over the world, including
30 between the towers of Sydney Harbour Bridge in Australia. His story has been the subject of plays and more recently, in 2008, director James March made a film about his life. The film was a huge success and received various awards.

1   What is the writer's main aim in writing the text?
  A   to talk about the things Philippe Petit has achieved
  B   to explain how to become a street entertainer
  C   to give information about some famous buildings
  D   to warn against the dangers of high-wire-walking

2   After Petit's arrest for his World Trade Centre stunt
  A   a politician told the police to release him.
  B   the crowd stopped the police from arresting him.
  C   nobody thought the stunt was against the law.
  D   the media interest became very important.

3   What would a reader learn about Philippe Petit from the text?
  A   He tries to avoid the media.
  B   He rarely plans his stunts.
  C   He has several performance skills.
  D   He dislikes very high buildings.

Vocabulary
Parts of the body

Read the definitions then rearrange the letters to find the words.

a between your hand and your arm   t r i s w   ....

b the things you see with   y s e e   ....

c used for picking things up   s g f i r n e   ....

d the thing you talk through   h t m u o   ....

e where your food goes to   c h s t m o a   ....

f what you use to run   s e l g   ....

g on the top of your body   d e a h   ....

h where your heart is   s e h c t   ....

Listening Part 2

▶2 You will hear someone talking on the radio about a film festival.
For questions 1–5, choose the correct answer A, B or C.

1 If you want to see more than one film, it's cheaper to
   A pay for each film you want to see.
   B get a weekend ticket.
   C buy one-day tickets.

2 How can people find out what films are being shown?
   A by getting a programme
   B by listening to the radio
   C by emailing the presenter

3 What does the presenter say about the
   version of *The Jungle Book* being shown?
   A It is better than the cartoon.
   B It will be popular with everybody.
   C It is a romantic film.

4 The presenter describes the 1986
   version of *The Fly* as
   A frightening.
   B original.
   C clever.

5 What is true about the filming of *Wolves:
   A Legend Returns to Yellowstone*?
   A Some filming is done from the air.
   B The cameramen get very close
      to the wolves.
   C All the shots are taken
      from long distance.

Grammar
Comparative and superlative adjectives

For a–h complete the second sentence so that it means the same as the first. Use no more than three words.

a Humans are more intelligent than animals.
  Animals aren't _____ as humans.

b Dogs are good pets in comparison to cats.
  Dogs are _____ than cats.

c Cheetahs are faster than any other animal in the world.
  Cheetahs are _____ animals in the world.

d Chimps and dolphins are both very clever.
  Chimps _____ as dolphins.

e Insects aren't as cute as some animals.
  Insects are _____ than some animals.

f Fish are easier to look after than other pets.
  Fish are the _____ pets to look after.

g Hippos are more dangerous than a lot of other animals.
  Hippos are one of _____ animals.

h Animals and humans are both equally important.
  Animals are _____ humans.

Vocabulary
Films

Say whether each sentence is true (T) or false (F). Check your answers in a dictionary.

a An **amusing** story is very funny. _____

b A **scary** story makes you feel frightened. _____

c An **amazing** film is usually a bit boring. _____

d A **brilliant** actor isn't very good. _____

e The **hero** of a story is male and the **heroine** is female. _____

f 'Graphics' is another word for the actors' lines. _____

g The **costumes** are what the actors wear. _____

h The **main character** in a film is always bad. _____

i A **scene** is the ending of a film. _____

j **Special effects** can include computer tricks. _____

Writing Part 2

You are going to get a new pet. Write an email to your English friend, Alice. In your email you should

➡ tell her what pet you are going to get

➡ say why you chose it

➡ suggest when you could meet

Write 35–45 words.

5 Health and sport

Vocabulary
Phrasal verbs

1 Match the phrasal verbs with meanings a–e.

| take up | throw away | get up |
| give up | cut down on | |

a
> to stop doing or having something that you did or had regularly before

b
> to get out of bed

c
> to get rid of rubbish or something that you do not want

d
> to start doing something regularly

e
> to reduce the quantity or amount of something

Grammar
The imperative

Rewrite the sentences using the imperative.

a You shouldn't eat unhealthy food.

....

b It's important not to smoke.

....

c Make sure you drink plenty of water.

....

d You should wear good-quality trainers.

....

e It's best to get to the gym early.

....

f It's best not to go to bed too late.

....

2 Complete these sentences with phrasal verbs from exercise 1 in the correct form.

a I .... at 7 a.m. every morning and then I have a shower.

b We're going to .... karate to get fit.

c Let's .... all the sweets and chocolates in the house and only eat healthy food!

d I'm going to .... fast food – I'll only have it twice a month.

e Last month my sister .... playing tennis and started doing basketball instead.

Reading Part 5

Read the text about Lewis Hamilton. For each question choose the correct answer, A, B, C or D.

Lewis Hamilton RACING STAR

Have you (1) .... dreamed about being a world-famous sports star? Lewis Hamilton, the British Formula One racing driver, has (2) .... written many books about his life and he has taken (3) .... in advertising campaigns. How did it all begin?

Lewis has driven racing cars (4) .... he was a teenager. Over the years he (5) .... lots of competitions, and was world champion in 2008. He has lived in Switzerland (6) .... many years now; his parents divorced when he was two and he (7) .... with his mother until he was ten. When Lewis was eight, his father (8) .... him a go-kart for Christmas. He took (9) .... go-karting at his local track, and showed great talent and determination. Eventually, he (10) .... up go-karting and joined the McLaren Young Driver Support Programme.

1 A ever	B yet	C never	D just
2 A yet	B just	C ever	D already
3 A out	B part	C up	D down
4 A for	B just	C since	D already
5 A win	B won	C has won	D is winning
6 A since	B for	C already	D from
7 A live	B was living	C lived	D has lived
8 A bought	B has bought	C to buy	D was buying
9 A out	B with	C away	D up
10 A made	B cut	C gave	D threw

Grammar

The present perfect

1 Complete the sentences with one of the verbs in the present perfect.

become	open	not see	finish	start	not ride

a I .... a horse before, but I have travelled on an elephant.
b The film .... Hurry up or you'll miss the beginning!
c Snowboarding .... very popular in recent years.
d The children .... their homework, so they can play football now.
e Marta .... the new *James Bond* film, but I have!
f A new swimming pool .... in our town.

2 Use the prompts to write questions and answers, as in the example.

Example

A *ever/ride/a motorbike*
B *never/ride/a motorbike/but/drive/a racing car*
A *Have you ever ridden a motorbike?*
B *I've never ridden a motorbike, but I've driven a racing car.*

1 **A** ever/see/a crocodile
  B never/see/a crocodile/but/hold/a snake

....

....

2 **A** ever/visit/Thailand
  B never/visit/Thailand/but/travel/ around India

....

....

3 **A** ever/fly/in a helicopter
  B never/fly/in a helicopter/but/be/in/ hot-air balloon

....

....

4 **A** ever/climb/a mountain
  B never/climb/a mountain/but/cross/ the Sahara Desert

....

....

3 Complete the sentences with *for* or *since*.

a I've wanted to be in the rugby team .... ages.

b My uncle's been a football manager .... two years.

c I've lived in this house .... I was born.

d My brother's been interested in sport .... he was very young.

e The boys have been in the park .... three hours.

f I've had my new mobile phone .... last weekend.

Vocabulary
Sport

Look at the words in a–f. Underline the odd word out in each group and say why it does not go with the others.

a	goalkeeper	baseball	referee	manager
b	mask	helmet	racket	pitch
c	boxing	scuba-diving	basket	athletics
d	kick	racket	throw	hit
e	pitch	court	track	goal
f	swimming	basketball	tennis	baseball

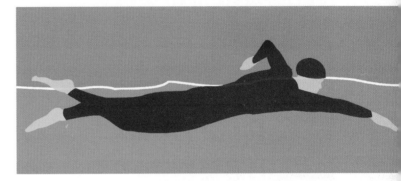

Writing Part 1

For a–h complete the second sentence so that it means the same as the first. Use no more than three words.

a It's a long time since I played basketball.
I .... basketball for a long time.

b They've just won the match.
They .... the match a few minutes ago.

c Our team needs to score a goal!
Our team .... a goal yet!

d I don't know how to play rugby.
I .... rugby before.

e I last went snowboarding in 2002.
I .... snowboarding since 2002.

f She's already been for a run today.
She .... for a run earlier today.

g She didn't pass her driving test yesterday.
She .... her driving test yet.

h He moved to London many years ago.
He .... in London for a long time.

6 Homes and lifestyles

Listening Part 3

▶3 You will hear a woman talking to a group of people about her houseboat.
For each question, fill in the missing information.

HOUSEBOAT TOURS

BACKGROUND

There are approximately (1) .... houseboats in Seattle.

The houseboat tour lasts (2) ....

Many of the houseboats have two or three (3) ....

Elizabeth Jones' houseboat

Rooms: bedroom; bathroom; kitchen; (4) ....

Other facilities: electricity; running water; the Internet

Elizabeth's book available from beginning of (5) ....

Grammar
The past perfect

1 Match the beginnings of the sentences 1–5 with endings a–f. There is one ending you do not need.

1 I had never been to Asia
2 We decided to learn English
3 When I arrived at the house
4 By the time she moved to Italy
5 My sister missed her flight

a because she had left her passport at home.
b she had been married for two years.
c when my parents had found jobs there.
d everyone else had gone out.
e until I went to Bangkok last year.
f after we had been offered jobs in New York.

2 Complete the sentences with the past perfect or the past simple form of the verbs in brackets.

a When I .... (arrive), the exam .... (already / start).
b I .... (never / see) a crocodile until I .... (go) to Egypt.
c The children went to the park because they .... (arrange) to meet some friends there.
d When I got home, I .... (discover) that I .... (lost) my bag.
e We .... (leave) the cinema before the film .... (end).
f After all the passengers .... (get) on the train, the doors .... (close).

Reading Part 3

Read the text about an unusual house in America and decide if each sentence (1–8) is correct or incorrect.

THE PYRAMID HOUSE

Harry Wilks, an American businessman, has built an unusual home in Ohio. The only part you can see is a giant blue pyramid-shaped window. The rest of the house is underground. The home is huge. It's around 2,000m² with a 760m² living
5 room that has enough space for about 80 guests. Of course, without a window above ground, the home would have little sunlight. The pyramid catches the maximum amount of natural light and softly lights up the rooms below.

The decoration of the room is as impressive as the design.
10 Wilks had been a keen collector of historic works of art before he even thought about building his home. Consequently, the house is filled with ancient things from Rome, Egypt, and Greece.

The world of art doesn't stop in Wilks' home. His house is
15 on top of a hill that's surrounded by forests and fields, and all around dotted across the countryside, are huge steel, bronze, and wooden sculptures. This is because The Pyramid House is in the middle of Pyramid Hill Sculpture Park and Museum. When the billionaire businessman first decided to build his home, he
20 fell in love with the beauty of the area and bought a lot of the surrounding land. Not knowing at first what to do with it, Harry decided to turn it into a sculpture park.

More than 100,000 people visit the park each year to enjoy the art and the scenery; others go to conferences, concerts,
25 weddings, and festivals there. Although Harry's house isn't open to the public, he has suggested that when he dies, it will become part of the sculpture park so that people will be able to see the personal and impressive museum collection inside.

1 None of Harry Wilks' house can be seen above ground.
2 Harry's house has plenty of room for entertaining people.
3 Harry's house is quite dark inside.
4 Harry has recently become interested in ancient history.
5 There are giant works of art just outside Harry's home.
6 The sculpture park existed before Harry built his house.
7 It's possible to listen to music at the sculpture park.
8 Visitors today are able to see Harry's own art collection.

Vocabulary
House and home

1 Write the answers using the words below.

balcony	countryside
kitchen	town
stairs	bungalow
city	hall
village	bathroom
flat	patio

a the room you usually cook in ....

b the part of a house that you first walk into ....

c four locations to live in

....

d two places attached to the outside of a house

....

e the part of the house that connects the ground floor with the top floors

....

f two types of home

....

g the room you usually wash in ....

2 Look at the words in a–e. Underline the odd one out in each group and give reasons why. Check your answers in a dictionary.

a	armchair	bookshelf	curtain	chest of drawers
b	basin	oven	bath	shower
c	ceiling	chimney	roof	fridge
d	pillow	cupboard	blanket	cushion
e	cellar	cottage	bedroom	study

Suffixes

Complete a–f with adjectives formed from the words in brackets.

a My little sister's very _____ (imagine). She's always making up games.

b It's a _____ (beauty) day. The sun is shining and the sky is blue.

c This film is _____ (bore). I feel like going to sleep.

d My parents recently bought a very _____ (comfort) new sofa.

e It's an _____ (interest) house. It looks a bit like a spaceship!

f My grandparents live in a _____ (wonder) cottage by the sea.

Negative prefixes

1 Write the opposites of the words below using *un*, *im* or *in*. Check your answers in a dictionary.

a expensive _____
b pleasant _____
c necessary _____
d convenient _____
e possible _____
f correct _____
g perfect _____
h fashionable _____

2 Complete the sentences with six words from exercise 1 or their negative form.

a What a(n) _____ dress! It looks like something people wore in the 1950s.

b The house may be lovely, but I'm afraid it's too _____ . We can't afford to buy it.

c I'm afraid it's a rather _____ time to phone. Could you call again later?

d I didn't enjoy that soup at all. It had a really _____ taste.

e All your answers in the test were _____ . I can't believe you did so badly!

f I can't do this exercise. It's _____ !

Writing Part 2

You are going to move to a new home. Write a card to your English friend, Carl. In your card you should

➡ describe your new home

➡ say when you are moving

➡ invite Carl to visit

Write 35–45 words.

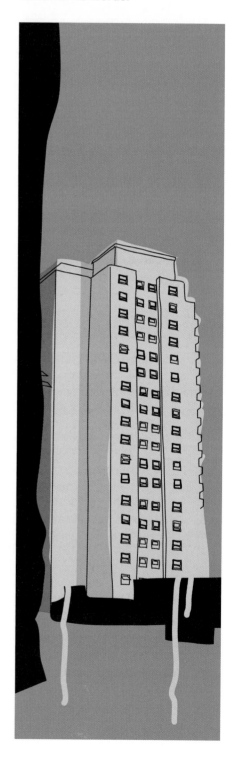

Review 2 Units 4–6

1 Read the text below and for 1–10 choose the correct answer A, B, C or D.

Healthy eating

People have been interested in good food (1)............ hundreds of years, but eating healthy food in the modern world is becoming difficult. This is because many of our foods contain artificial flavours and colours which are bad for us. So what can we do? First, look in your cupboards and throw (2)............ anything that isn't healthy! Then, try to choose the food you buy more carefully. It's (3)............ to eat organic fruit and vegetables. However, these can be more expensive (4)............ other products and not everybody can afford them. If you can't buy organic products, the (5)............ thing you can do is to read food labels and check what ingredients are in the food. It's (6)............ to avoid artificial products all the time, but there are other things you can do. You (7)............ drink plenty of water and eat lots of fruit and vegetables. Cut (8)............ on fried and rich foods that contain lots of fats, sugar and white flour. (9)............ buying ready-made food and fast food and you should feel great and look (10)............ too!

1	A since	B yet	C for	D just
2	A up	B on	C away	D across
3	A healthier	B healthily	C more healthier	
	D most healthiest			
4	A as	B than	C with	D to
5	A good	B well	C best	D better
6	A uncomfortable	B imperfect	C incorrect	
	D impossible			
7	A would	B should	C may	D ought
8	A down	B out	C up	D across
9	A Avoided	B Avoid	C To avoid	D Avoiding
10	A amusing	B pleasant	C amazing	D convenient

2 Complete the second sentence so that it means the same as the first. Use no more than three words.

a It's a long time since they saw Jack.
They .... Jack for a long time.

b This is the first time I've been surfing.
I .... surfing before.

c We went to the supermarket this morning.
We .... to the supermarket already.

d There was nobody at the party when I arrived.
By the time I arrived at the party everybody .... home.

e No one in the class is taller than Claudia.
Claudia is .... person in the class.

f Swimming in a pool isn't as good as swimming in the sea.
Swimming in the sea .... swimming in a pool.

g Is he the oldest person in the world?
Is anyone in the world .... is?

h He saw what the letter said, then burned it.
After he .... what the letter said, he burned it.

3 For a–h choose the correct words to complete the sentences.

a A *bungalow / house* usually has stairs.

b Haven't you heard the news *already / yet*?

c A *goalkeeper / referee* usually saves goals.

d You usually find a village in the *city / countryside*.

e She's bought some new *curtains / cushions* for the kitchen window.

f We can see the whole city from our *cellar / balcony*.

g You need a racket to play *tennis / baseball*.

h Most horror films are too *amusing / scary* for me to watch!

Reading Part 4

Read the text about an artist. For questions 1–4 choose the correct answer A, B, C or D.

A Different Kind Of Art

Artist Adrian Gray is an unusual kind of artist. He makes shapes by balancing stones. He first discovered stone balancing when he was making sculptures out of stone on a beach one day. He accidentally balanced one stone on
5 another in what seemed an impossible way.

Adrian has always been interested in stones. He was born in Bristol in the south of England. He studied geology and spent a long time travelling, studying and photographing stones in places like the Himalayas and around the Pacific.
10 A tropical illness caused him to stop travelling and to settle back in Britain. He chose to live in a small seaside town and began to develop his art of stone balancing.

Adrian displays his art for local people and visitors to see. Most of the people who see Adrian's work are amazed.
15 They cannot believe that it's possible to balance rocks on such a small point of contact. They often believe that he's using glue or magnets of some kind. So, how do the stones balance? It seems that it's all to do with physics. Gravity and friction cause the stones to stay in place.

20 Adrian's works of art take different lengths of time to complete. Some can take a few seconds or minutes while others take days. Of course Adrian's works do not last long. A gust of wind, a wave or a downfall of rain can cause the stones to suddenly fall. That's why he has a
25 camera set up at all times so that he can take photos of his work before it disappears. Adrian sells these photos to make a living. He also works as a stonemason and a roofer, and makes bird tables and chests out of driftwood.

1 What is the writer's main aim in writing the text?
   A to describe the changing career of an artist
   B to show how to make different types of sculpture
   C to talk about the benefits of being an artist by the sea
   D to explain the secrets of an artist's work

2 What would a reader learn about Adrian Gray from the text?
   A He has many different skills.
   B He prefers working with wood.
   C He has always worked artistically with stones.
   D He brought back many stones from the Himalayas.

3 What does the writer say about Adrian's works of art?
   A They always take hours to create.
   B They are often destroyed by the weather.
   C They are sometimes fixed with glue.
   D They are unpopular with tourists.

4 Which of the following could also be a title for this text?
   A The tricks and secrets of stone balancing
   B Using natural resources for art
   C Taking photos of people and stones
   D Different ways to make money from art

Vocabulary
Materials

Match the different materials with a–h.

| plastic | metal | glass | wool |
| leather | wood | cotton | paper |

a   Windows are usually made from this. ....

b   This natural material comes from sheep. ....

c   You make clothes such as dresses and shirts from this material. ....

d   Most books are made using this. ....

e   A strong man-made material that's used to make many children's toys. ....

f   It is used for the main parts of cars, planes and other machines. ....

g   A natural material that comes from trees. ....

h   Your shoes may be made from this material. ....

Grammar
Order of adjectives

1   Underline the adjectives in a–f, then write them in the correct place on the chart below.

a   a lovely tiny glass ornament

b   an incredible old china vase

c   a circular brown wooden table

d   a pair of white Italian leather shoes

e   a pair of long rectangular metal earrings

f   an amazing ancient Egyptian monument

	Opinion	Size	Age	Shape	Colour	Nationality	Material
a							
b							
c							
d							
e							
f							

2   Rewrite any incorrect sentences, putting the adjectives into the correct order.

a   My parents have bought a lovely modern oval table.

b   Anna's wearing a beautiful silk black dress.

c   I bought a tiny glass purple figure of a cat for my mother's birthday.

d   We saw a very modern Russian interesting version of *Romeo and Juliet*.

e   The walls of our new house are painted a horrible dark-green colour.

f   I went to a 12th century fascinating castle at the weekend.

Vocabulary
Entertainment

Match the words with definitions a–f. There are three words you don't need.

audience	stage	performance
exit	costume	actresses
scene	entrance	play

a a platform in a theatre, concert hall, etc. on which actors, musicians, etc. perform

b one part of a book, play, film, etc. in which the events happen in one place

c the act of coming or going into a place, especially in a way that attracts attention

d a piece of writing performed by actors in the theatre, or on TV or radio

e all the people who are watching or listening to a play, concert, speech, the TV, etc.

f clothes that an actor, etc. wears in order to look like someone else

Grammar
Gerunds and infinitives

1 Choose the correct form of the verbs in italics to complete the sentences.

a We can't afford *to go/going* on holiday this year.

b Can you imagine *to be/being* a famous actor?

c I really enjoy *to play/playing* basketball.

d The children didn't manage *to finish/finishing* all the sandwiches on their picnic.

e Where do you suggest *meeting/to meet* later?

f I refuse *to wait/waiting* ages for a bus. I'd rather walk.

g Have you decided *to study/studying* languages at university?

h Would you consider *to become/becoming* a teacher?

2 Complete sentences a–e with one of the prepositions, and one of the verbs in the gerund.

| of | before | after | about | in |
| go | eat | play | get | join |

a I usually read the newspaper reviews _____ to see a new film at the cinema.

b I sometimes feel ill _____ seafood.

c My sister's thinking _____ a job picking fruit in France this summer.

d Marc's mad _____ the guitar.

e Are you interested _____ a band?

Writing Part 3

1 Read the task below and Isabella's letter. Which piece of information does she leave out?

This is part of a letter you receive from an English penfriend.

In your next letter, please tell me about a film you've seen recently. What's it about? Who plays the main character? What's your favourite part of the film?

Now write a letter answering your penfriend's questions.

Dear Anna

Thanks for your letter. You asked me about a film I saw recently. I went to see the comedy *Night at the Museum 2* last week.

The film is about a museum where the exhibits come to life at night. In the first film the hero, Larry Daley, who is played by Ben Stiller, is a security man at the museum. In this film he has a different job, but he returns to help his friends when they are in trouble.

You should watch the film because it's funny, although it isn't as good as the first one.

See you soon!

Isabella

2 Write your own answer to the task in exercise 1. Write about 100 words.

8 Safety

Reading Part 1

Read texts 1–4 and choose A, B or C.

1

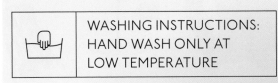

A You should avoid using a washing machine.
B You should avoid using cold water.
C You should avoid washing this item.

2

A You shouldn't use soap to clean this kettle.
B You should only ever wash the outside of this kettle.
C You shouldn't use this kettle without washing it first.

3

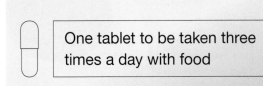

A Take these tablets during mealtimes.
B Take these tablets every day for three days.
C Take three tablets each time you eat.

4

NO PARKING IN FRONT OF GATES

ENTRANCE REQUIRED AT ALL TIMES

A Drivers never use this entrance.
B Drivers may only stop here for a short time.
C Drivers aren't allowed to stop here.

Grammar
Obligation, prohibition and necessity

Read sentences a–h about being a taxi driver. Correct the mistake in each one. There may be more than one possible answer.

a You needn't know your way around the city very well.
b You mustn't be a sociable person, but it helps!
c You don't need to be a safe driver.
d You haven't got to have a driving licence.
e You must drive if you're not feeling well.
f You have to own your own cab, you can work for a company.
g You must drive over the speed limit.
h You need satellite navigation but it could be useful.

Vocabulary
Household objects

1 Look at pictures 1–10. Match them with descriptions a–j and name the objects. Check your answers in a dictionary.

a you use it for opening bottles ....
b it keeps you cool in hot weather ....
c you dry plates, etc. with this ....
d you heat it and use it to flatten your clothes

....

e you keep this outside for putting rubbish in

....

f you put oil in it and cook in it ....
g you can carry water in this ....
h you drink from this and it's bigger than a cup

....

i you put flowers in it ....
j you turn it on to give light ....

2 Choose the correct answer for these questions.

a What do you use for eating soup: a **fork** or a **spoon**?
b What's the best way to boil potatoes: in a **kettle** or in a **saucepan**?
c Would you drink juice from a **glass** or a **plate**?
d Are the bags you get from a supermarket made of **china** or **plastic**?
e What do you usually drink coffee from: a **cup** or a **jug**?
f What's a knife usually made of: **wood** or **metal**?

Grammar
Ability and possibility

Choose the correct verbs to complete the sentences. Write A for ability or P for possibility.

a We *might / can* go on holiday to Italy, but it's not certain. ....
b *Can / Might* you explain this question to me? ....
c I *can't / may not* answer this question. It's too hard. ....
d There *can / could* be a storm later this afternoon. ....
e I *can't / might* call you until 3pm because I'm going to the dentist's after lunch. ....
f I *may / can* see you tomorrow night at the concert, but I haven't got a ticket yet.

....

g I *might / can* have enough money to go shopping tomorrow. ....
h He's so bad at cooking that he *can't / could* cook pasta! ....

Listening Part 1

▶4 **For 1–5 choose the correct picture, A, B or C.**

1 What will the weather be like later today?

A   B   C

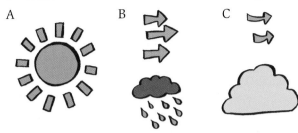

2 Who called the emergency services?

A   B   C

3 How did the fire start?

A   B   C

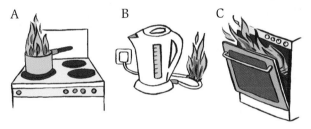

4 Where did the man leave the shopping?

A   B   C

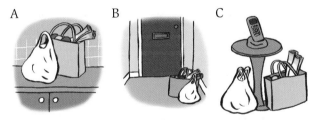

5 How did the woman find out about
   Anna's accident?

A   B   C

Vocabulary
The weather

Look at the weather reports and for a–h write
T (True) or F (False).

10°C	20°C	30°C	12°C
LONDON	ROME	CAIRO	PARIS
-10°C	8°C	FOG 9°C	25°C
MOSCOW	EDINBURGH	DUBLIN	TOKYO

a It's cool and rainy in London.   ....

b It's sunny and dry in Rome.   ....

c It's freezing in Cairo.   ....

d It's cloudy and cool in Paris.   ....

e It's snowy in Moscow.   ....

f It's boiling in Edinburgh.   ....

g It's warm and dry in Dublin.   ....

h It's foggy in Tokyo.   ....

Writing Part 2

**You have had an accident and can't go to
your friend's party. Write a card to your friend.
In your card you should**

➡ describe how the accident happened

➡ say how you are now

➡ suggest when you could meet again

Write 35–45 words.

Reading Part 3

Read the text about a female astronaut and decide if each sentence (1–8) is correct or incorrect.

THE FIRST FEMALE SPACE TOURIST

On September 18, 2006, Anousheh Ansari became only the fourth private space explorer ever and the first female one. In addition, she
5 was also the first astronaut of Iranian descent.

Anousheh has had an amazing life. She emigrated to the United States when she was a teenager,
10 and at the time she could speak no English. Despite this, she learned the language, studied hard and showed a talent for science and technology. She got a degree in electronics and computer
15 engineering, followed by a master's degree in electrical engineering. When she left university, she rapidly achieved one of her dreams by creating a multi-million-dollar business.

When Anousheh went on her amazing journey, she
20 achieved another one of her dreams. As a child she had always dreamed of being an astronaut and exploring space. Before her eight-day expedition, Anousheh prepared for her trip by having cosmonaut training at the Yuri Gagarin Cosmonaut Training Center in Star
25 City, Russia. As well as theory and physical training,

she also learned to speak some Russian. She then joined the International Space Station as part of the *Expedition 14* crew, which included Spanish–American
30 astronaut Michael Lopez-Alegria and Russian cosmonaut Mikhail Tyurin.

Unlike her predecessors, while she was in space, Anousheh wrote an Internet diary, which was read by
35 thousands of people back on earth. She described how she felt on the days before the flight, and her stay on board the space station. She talked about the sights and smells around her, and ordinary
40 activities like eating and washing-up – but in zero gravity! While she was on the space station, Anousheh also did various experiments for the European Space Agency. She conducted experiments into the effects of space travel on the crew members' health, and made a
45 study of space station microbes.

Back on earth, Anousheh has returned to her work with her companies, but she is still very much a part of the space programme. One of her dreams is to encourage young people around the world, especially girls, to
50 follow their dreams.

1 Anousheh Ansari was the first private explorer in space.
2 Anousheh learned English while living in Iran.
3 One of Anousheh's dreams was to be successful in business.
4 Anousheh's space trip lasted for less than a week.
5 Anousheh speaks at least three languages.
6 Anousheh stayed on the space station with an all-American crew.
7 Anousheh talked about daily events in her online diary.
8 Anousheh is no longer involved in space projects.

Grammar
The passive

Complete the text with the correct active or passive form of the verbs given.

Recycling Mobile Phones

In the 1970s, the first mobile phones (1) .... (make) in the United States. Today, millions of people (2) .... (own) a mobile phone. Technology is always improving, and every year over 15 million phones (3) .... (replace) by their owners. It (4) .... (estimate) that there are now over three billion phones. The problem is that around 90 million of them (5) .... (not use). Many (6) .... (leave) in drawers and cupboards until they (7) .... (throw) away.

One way we can help is to donate these phones to charities that (8) .... (send) relief workers to disaster areas. In 2000, mobile phones (9) .... (use) to help organise aid during the Mozambique floods. They (10) .... (also / give) to relief workers during the earthquakes in El Salvador and India.

Vocabulary
Technology

1 Complete the sentences with six of the words below.

text	keyboard	mouse	Internet
screen	laptop	calculator	software

a You type information into a computer using the ....

b Special .... is available to help you design a website.

c You use a .... to move around a computer screen.

d A .... can be useful if you want to work while you are travelling.

e You use a .... to solve maths problems.

f You can see the work you are doing by looking at the computer ....

2 Choose the correct verb for each sentence. Check your answers in a dictionary.

a When you finish talking to someone on the phone you *hang up/turn up*.

b If you want to take something off your computer, you *enter/delete* it.

c First you pick up your phone, then you *connect/dial* the number.

d To open something on your computer, you usually *enter/click* on it.

e If you can't *connect/dial* to the Internet, phone your Internet provider.

f You need to *click/enter* your credit card details before you can buy the product.

Grammar
Agreeing and disagreeing

Complete the dialogues with *so do/am/would I* or *neither do/am/would I*.

> **1** **Ben:** I think technology is a good thing.
> **Sue:** ...., but I also think people should be sensible and recycle their machines and devices.
> **Ben:** .... It's really important.

> **2** **Jill:** I don't think you should buy a new computer.
> **Paolo:** .... because I haven't got enough money. Anyway, I think people replace their computers too often.
> **Jill:** .... It just isn't necessary.

> **3** **Maria:** I'd like to go to that new museum.
> **Dan:** ...., but I'm hungry.
> **Maria:** Yeah, ... Let's have something to eat and go later.

> **4** **Hans:** I'm not interested in science subjects.
> **Tina:** .... I prefer languages.
> **Hans:** .... I want to do French and Spanish at university.

Vocabulary

Work and jobs

1 Write the answers using the words below.

writer	photographer	lorry driver
dancer	comedian	waiter	artist
designer	actor

a someone who travels long distances in a vehicle

....

b three people who might perform on stage

....

c someone who serves in a cafe or restaurant

....

d someone who has new ideas for clothes, the inside of buildings, etc. ....

e two people who create pictures ....

....

f someone who produces novels, articles, short stories, etc. ....

2 Write the names of the jobs using the words below with the correct ending.

| politics | library | music | science |
| direct | produce | instruct | sail |

a A(n) .... helps govern the country.

b A(n) .... works in a place where people borrow books.

c A(n) .... manages or controls a company or organisation.

d A(n) .... is a person that makes or grows something.

e A(n) .... is someone that studies a subject like chemistry or biology.

f A(n) .... is a person who teaches a practical skill or sport.

g A(n) .... works on a boat or ship.

h A(n) .... plays an instrument for a living.

Writing Part 1

For a–e complete the second sentence so that it means the same as the first. Use no more than three words.

a They sell digital cameras in the electrical store.
Digital cameras .... in the electrical store.

b They grow olives in countries like Greece and Italy.
Olives .... in countries like Greece and Italy.

c People in China invented the first paper.
The first paper .... in China.

d Millions of people watch the World Cup every four years.
The World Cup .... millions of people every four years.

e Somebody stole ten computers from our school last night.
Ten computers .... from our school last night.

Vocabulary
Personality adjectives

Match sentences 1–8 with a–h below.

1　My brother is lazy.
2　Max is selfish.
3　My new boyfriend's funny.
4　Sam is so bossy.
5　My dad is very generous.
6　George is sociable.
7　My cousin's reliable.
8　My uncle's brave.

a　He makes me laugh a lot.
b　He once saved some people from a fire.
c　He loves to go out and to meet people.
d　He never thinks about other people.
e　He gives things to people all the time.
f　He always does what he says he'll do.
g　He gets up late and never does any work.
h　He's always telling people what to do.

Phrasal verbs with *get*

Match the phrasal verbs in bold in 1–8 with meanings a–h. Check your answers in a dictionary.

1　I **get on** with everyone in my family.
2　When did you **get back** from your holiday?
3　Please **get down** from that ladder! It looks dangerous.
4　Let's **get in** the car and leave.
5　You need to **get off** at the next stop.
6　My sister's going away to **get over** her failed relationship.
7　You should **get rid of** that old TV and buy a new one.
8　What time do you usually **get up** in the morning?

a　to leave a bus, train, etc.
b　to return to the place where you live or work
c　to deal with a problem successfully
d　to have a friendly relationship with someone
e　to throw away something you don't want
f　to return to the ground from a high place
g　to climb into something
h　to get out of bed

Listening Part 4

▶5 You will hear a conversation between a girl, Jess, and a boy, Billy, about their plans for the weekend. Decide if each sentence is correct or incorrect.

1　Billy is planning to leave his job soon.
2　Jess thinks going to the nightclub is a good idea.
3　Billy gets on well with all his family.
4　Billy is going to sleep at his parents' house on Saturday night.
5　Jess suggests going to the cinema the following week.

Reading Part 1

1 Read messages 1–4 and write in the missing words.

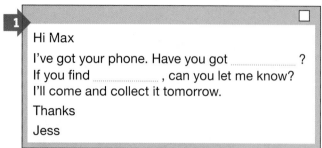

1 ☐

Hi Max

I've got your phone. Have you got _____ ?
If you find _____ , can you let me know?
I'll come and collect it tomorrow.

Thanks

Jess

2 ☐

Josh

_____ party is on Saturday now, not
Friday. _____ starts at 8 and ends late!
Can _____ still bring your CDs?

Ben

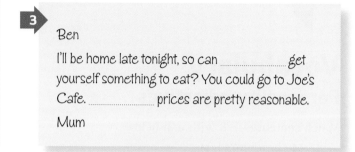

3

Ben

I'll be home late tonight, so can _____ get
yourself something to eat? You could go to Joe's
Cafe. _____ prices are pretty reasonable.

Mum

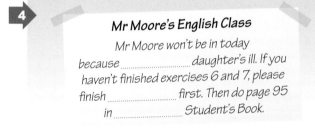

4

Mr Moore's English Class

Mr Moore won't be in today
because _____ daughter's ill. If you
haven't finished exercises 6 and 7, please
finish _____ first. Then do page 95
in _____ Student's Book.

2 Read the complete messages in Exercise 1 again.
Decide what each one says and choose A, B or C.

1 Jess wants Max to
  A send back her phone.
  B look for her phone.
  C lend her a phone.

2 Why has Ben sent a message to Josh?
  A to invite him to his party
  B to tell him something has changed
  C to remind him about something

3 Why has Mum left this message for Ben?
  A to tell him to meet her at Joe's Cafe
  B to ask him to bring her something to eat
  C to explain that he needs to buy some food

4 The purpose of the message is to
  A say that Mr Moore has been delayed.
  B explain that the English class is cancelled.
  C give instructions to the students.

Grammar
The future

1 Choose the correct future form to complete each sentence.

a '*I meet / I'm going to meet* James at six o'clock this evening.'

b Oh no, it's raining. The picnic *is / is going to be* cancelled!

c The train *will leave / leaves* at 2 o'clock from platform eight.

d 'My bag's so heavy.' '*I'll carry / I carry* it for you.'

e I'm sure that one day *I am / I'll be* rich and famous.

f 'I'm going into town later.' 'Are you? *I'm going to come / I'll come* with you then.'

2 Match sentences a–f in exercise 1 with 1–6 below.

1 general prediction

2 plan / intention

3 timetable / schedule

4 offer

5 prediction based on evidence

6 decision made at the time of speaking / writing

3 Read Robbie's email to Max, then complete 1–6 with the correct future form of the verbs in brackets.

Hi Max

I just wanted to tell you about my holiday arrangements and to see what you're doing tonight!

I (1) .... (visit) my grandparents next week and then we (2) .... (go) to the seaside together. We (3) .... (meet) my aunt and uncle down there. We (4) .... (probably / be) there for a couple of weeks, because my aunt and uncle have got an apartment.

Anyway I'm free this evening, so do you fancy going to the cinema? There's a good film on in town. It (5) .... (start) at seven. I (6) .... (pay) if you like – I know you haven't got any money.

See you later!

Robbie

Writing Part 2

You are having a party. Write a card to your English friend, Belinda. In your card you should

➡ explain why you are having the party

➡ tell her when and where it is

➡ say who will be there

Write 35–45 words.

Review 3 Units 7–10

1 Read the text below and for 1–10 choose the correct answer A, B, C or D.

Cloud forests

Cloud forests (1)_____ in tropical mountains. Most of them are in Asia, but they are also in Latin America and Africa. Cloud forests (2)_____ water from the clouds and the fog and this produces clean water supplies for people in many areas. The cloud forests of La Tigra National Park in Honduras (3)_____ over 40% of the water for around 850,000 people. The problem is that scientists think that cloud forests will one day (4)_____. Part of the reason for this is that people are (5)_____ rid of large sections of the forests for farming and road-building. However, scientists think that climate change (6)_____ be the biggest danger. Warmer temperatures might (7)_____ the clouds lift and the forests will dry out. Conservation groups have decided (8)_____ protect the rainforests, but all of us (9)_____ think about global warming and its effects. Anyone interested (10)_____ the future of the cloud forests can contact their local environment group.

1 A are found   B find   C are finding
  D have found
2 A are taking   B are taken   C take
  D have taken
3 A were provided   B provide   C are provided
  D providing
4 A disappear   B disappearing   C disappeared
  D to disappear
5 A making   B having   C doing   D getting
6 A would   B can   C should   D could
7 A making   B make   C made   D to make
8 A help   B to help   C helping   D to helping
9 A need   B might   C may   D must
10 A of   B for   C in   D from

2 For a–j choose the correct word or phrase to complete the sentence.

a How many different species of animals *find/are found* in rainforests?
b The pen *did invented/was invented* by the ancient Egyptians.
c 'I enjoy learning about the environment.' '*So/Neither* do I.'
d 'I don't use the Internet every day.' '*So/Neither* do I.'
e *I'm meeting/I'll meet* some friends this afternoon.
f 'I don't like this sandwich.' '*I'll eat/I'm going to eat* it if you don't want it!'
g The bus to town *leaves/will leave* at three o'clock every afternoon.
i You *don't have to/don't ought to* exercise every day.
j We *could not/can't* go to Greece next year, I'm afraid.
k Drivers *might/must* always stop at a red light.

3 Decide whether sentences a–h are true (T) or false (F).

a If it's foggy, it can be difficult to see.
b If you are selfish, you always think about other people.
c Actors perform on a scene.
d When you finish a phone call, you hang up.
e You can use a vase to boil water.
f Boots are often made of leather.
g You usually find a jug in a kitchen.
h A bossy person asks other people what to do.

11 The natural world

Reading Part 2

1 The people in 1–3 all want to do something to help the environment. Read the descriptions and texts A–E and decide which option would be the most suitable for them.

1 Anna and Mario have just finished their school exams and they want to do something challenging before they go to university. They're interested in travelling as well as doing something positive for the environment.

2 James works in an office from 9–5, but wants to make some extra money as he's planning to go abroad for a year. He enjoys being in the fresh air and likes travelling.

3 Dana is looking for a job with a charity. She is happy to work either full-time or part-time in an office environment. She wants to be based locally, but is willing to travel occasionally.

FUND-RAISERS REQUIRED
FOR ANIMAL CONSERVATION GROUP.

The position requires three full days per week at our main building. Also requires two or three trips abroad per year.

B

Part-time workers required for weekend and evening work on

Hartwell's Organic Farm.

We are looking for people to work in the fields and to deliver goods to customers in the area. Vans provided.

C

FED UP WITH SEEING LITTER EVERYWHERE? WANT TO DO SOMETHING ABOUT IT?

We need volunteers to spend the day picking up litter on our local beach. If you would like to help, meet 9am on Saturday 25th June at the open-air pool.

D

eco-living magazine

Interested in writing? We pay good money to freelance writers for our new green magazine *Eco-living*. Articles on organic farming and eco-friendly cars are especially welcome for next month's issue.

E

Would you like to make a difference to the

Amazon Rainforest?

We are looking for volunteers to work for six-month periods on a variety of projects. Flights and accommodation provided, and an opportunity to work on a project in a different country afterwards.

Vocabulary
Prepositions

Read the text below and correct six of the prepositions in **bold**.

Litter on Ben Nevis

Conservationists and volunteers are all involved (1) **with** trying to clear litter from Britain's highest mountain, Ben Nevis. The litter, which consists (2) **on** tents, bottles, equipment, food packaging, and even a piano, has been blamed (3) **after** lazy climbers who don't believe (4) **on** looking after the environment. Volunteer organisations have already taken steps to protect the mountain (5) **from** further damage. They encourage climbers to take their rubbish home with them. Other countries insist (6) **in** this by asking for money if climbers do not pick up their litter. By doing this, they are hoping (7) **for** a cleaner mountain in the future. If you want to learn more (8) **of** the conservation efforts taking place on Ben Nevis, you can find plenty of information online.

Grammar
Zero and first conditional

Read a–h and decide if they are zero or first conditional sentences. Then complete them with the correct form of the verb in brackets.

a If we don't look after our environment, temperatures .... (rise).

b You save electricity if you .... (turn) off lights and other electrical equipment.

c We .... (not have) any oil left for the future if we use it all now.

d If we .... (not stop) cutting down trees, we'll lose many species of animal.

e There .... (not be) any mountain gorillas left unless people stop hunting them.

f The rainforests will have a better chance of survival if we .... (look) after them.

g If you .... (put) on a jumper, not the heating, you'll save money on bills.

h Eat organic food if you .... (want) to avoid harmful chemicals.

Second conditional

Find the mistake in each second conditional sentence and rewrite the sentence correctly.

a If my sister has a degree, she'd love to work in animal conservation.

....
....

b My parents wouldn't drive a car if public transport would be more reliable.

....
....

c If I am very rich, I'd plant a forest of trees.

....
....

d I won't ride a motorbike if I were you.

....
....

e If I have climbed a mountain, I wouldn't leave any rubbish there.

....
....

f People would respect the environment more if they are fined for damaging it.

....
....

Vocabulary

Phrasal verbs

1 Choose the correct words in italics to complete the phrasal verbs in a–f. Check your answers in a dictionary.

  a You should always pick *on/up/down* your litter and take it home.

  b One day the world will run *for/out/up* of oil.

  c I'm going to give *up/out/in* eating meat and become a vegetarian.

  d You should always turn *off/out/up* the TV when you leave the room.

  e Don't turn *down/out/on* the light! It isn't even dark yet.

  f Can you fill *out/in/up* that vase with water so I can put these flowers in it?

2 Match the answers to exercise 1 with these meanings.

1	to become or to make something become completely full
2	to stop doing or having something that you did or had regularly before
3	to take hold of and lift something
4	to stop the flow of electricity, water, etc. by moving a switch, tap, etc.
5	to finish a supply of something
6	to start the flow of electricity, water, etc. by moving a switch, tap, etc.

Writing Part 2

1 Read the task and the answers A–C below, ignoring the spelling and punctuation mistakes. Which answer includes all the required information?

You are working as a volunteer in another country. Write an email to an English friend, Tom. In your email, you should

➡ tell him where you are
➡ describe what work you are doing
➡ suggest meeting in the future

Write 35–45 words.

A ☐
Hi Tom

I'm working as a volunteer and I'm having a fantastic time. Iv'e met so many intresting people. Lets meet when I next come to London. We could go for a meal or something.

See you soon!

Isabella

B ☐
Hi Tom

Guess what? I'm working as a volunteer, studying the diffrent plant forms here. I'll be here for about six months and then Im meeting some friends in Rio de Janeiro.

hope to see you soon!

Carmen

C ☐
Hi Tom

I'm working as a volunteer in the Brazilian rainforest at the moment. I'm involved in a project that studies different species of bird. I'm hear until september and then I'm in England. Shall we meet in London some time!

Bye!

Jasmine

2 Find and correct three mistakes with spelling or punctuation in each answer in exercise 1.

3 Write your own answer to the task in exercise 1.

12 ▶ Food and celebrations

Vocabulary
Food and drink

1 Complete the names of these foods.

a Dairy:
  m.........k
  c h.....................
  b...............................

b Protein:
  n......t
  f.........h
  c.......................e n

c Vegetables:
  ....r r.....t
  p e..........
  o n..............

d Fruit:
  b..................n.......
  a.....p.........
  g r...............

2 Look at the words in a–h. Underline the odd word out in each group and explain why. Check your answers in a dictionary.

a bake	grill	steak	roast
b coconut	lemon	honey	melon
c cabbage	cauliflower	carrot	cereal
d tuna	chicken	duck	lamb
e mustard	mushroom	pepper	salt
f lettuce	jam	cucumber	tomato
g slice	cup	bowl	saucepan
h spoon	toast	fork	chopsticks

Grammar
Comparative and superlative adverbs

Read sentences a–h and correct any mistakes with adverbs.

a My brother cooks best than anyone else in our house.

b Mario speaks English the most fluently in our class.

c My father drives as carefully as my mother.

d I dress more smart than usual when I go to a wedding.

e I play basketball as well than my friends. In fact, I'm probably better.

f I eat fast food less often than I used to.

g I worked the most hard in our class this year.

h I'm as tall as everybody else in my class.

Reading Part 3

Read the text about Independence Day celebrations in America and decide if each sentence (1–6) is correct or incorrect.

YOU'LL SIMPLY ♥ NY

Are you planning a trip to New York City? If you're interested in festivals and celebrations, a good time to go is around 4th July. This is Independence Day in America. It's a national holiday celebrating the day in 1776 when the USA became
5 independent from Britain. During this holiday period there are traditional parades, barbecues, carnivals, picnics, concerts and baseball games everywhere. The streets are decorated with red, white and blue balloons and streamers, political figures give important speeches and there are firework displays.

10 If you're interested in seeing a parade, try going to Travis, which is an area located on the West Shore of Staten Island. If you don't already know, Staten Island is a borough in New York City. It's separated from the city by a stretch of water called New York Bay, so remember you'll need to get the ferry across!
15 The Travis parade consists of marching bands, people dancing, colourful costumes and of course lots of flag waving. The parade starts at 12.30 pm, whatever the weather, but roads are closed one hour before.

America's most exciting 4th July firework display also takes
20 place in New York City and is organised by Macy's, the famous department store. The display starts at around 9 pm with fireworks being released from boats along the Hudson River. There is also live music by well-known bands. If you're driving, you need to be careful because some parts of the city are
25 closed to traffic during the day. Check local tourist offices or the websites to find out exactly where to get the best view of the fireworks. You can also go on a cruise on a water taxi to view the fireworks. Prices vary depending on whether you're planning to have a meal and whether you want live
30 entertainment – again check the websites.

1 The 4th July celebrations involve music and sport.
2 You can travel to the Travis parade by boat.
3 The Travis parade only takes place in good weather.
4 Macy's firework display begins on the streets of the city.
5 You can drive around some parts of New York on 4th July.
6 All boat trips on 4th July cost the same.

Listening Part 2

▶ 6 You will hear someone interviewing a woman called Josie on a food programme. For questions 1–5, choose the correct answer A, B or C.

1 Josie's parents preferred cooking recipes
   A from different countries.
   B with lots of ingredients.
   C that were simple to prepare.

2 What happened to Josie at college?
   A She left before the end of the course.
   B She only enjoyed some parts of the course.
   C She completed the course successfully.

3 What did Josie dislike about working at the restaurant?
   A the people she worked with
   B the speed of the job
   C the type of food she had to cook

4 When did Josie start writing articles about food?
   A after a bad experience at a restaurant
   B during her journalism course
   C when she applied for a job with a magazine

5 What are Josie's plans for the future?
   A to set up her own magazine
   B to buy a restaurant
   C to stop work for a year

Grammar
Reported speech

1 Rewrite the dialogues in 1–5 in reported speech, as in the example.

Ben: Give me my pen!
Joe: Don't be so rude!

Example
Ben told Joe to give him his pen.
Joe told Ben not to be so rude.

> **1** | **Mum:** | What did you eat at school?
> | **Sam:** | I had a sandwich.
>
> ....
> ....

> **2** | **Liz:** | Are you hungry?
> | **Tom:** | Yes. Do you want to go to the cafe?
>
> ....
> ....

> **3** | **Anna:** | Don't touch my phone!
> | **David:** | Sorry! I didn't know it was yours.
>
> ....
> ....

> **4** | **Mick:** | What's your favourite food?
> | **Jessica:** | I like everything!
>
> ....
> ....

> **5** | **Millie:** | Tell me a story, dad!
> | **Dad:** | All right. Do you want a fairy tale?
>
> ....
> ....

2 Complete the sentences with *say*, *ask* or *tell* in the past simple.

a I .... that I preferred fish to meat.
b Pat .... his mum that he didn't like eggs.
c The waitress .... us if we wanted dessert.
d Isabelle .... me that she was hungry.
e Olivia .... that she was enjoying her meal.
f The teacher angrily .... the student not to be rude.
g We were lost, so we .... a man where the restaurant was.
h The children .... that they had eaten enough.

Vocabulary
Tastes

Underline the correct adjectives to describe the foods in a–g.

a Crisps are *sour / sweet / salty*.
b Strong coffee can be *bitter / spicy / sour*.
c Seafood tastes *fishy / sweet / bitter*.
d Lemons are *salty / sour / sweet*.
e Chocolate cake is *sweet / spicy / salty*.
f Chillies are usually *hot / sweet / bitter*.
g Curry is usually *bitter / sour / spicy*.

Writing Part 3

1 Match the titles of the stories with endings a–e. There is one extra ending you don't need.

1 The kindest person in the world
2 A miserable day
3 A fantastic meal
4 The amazing journey

a We paid the bill and told the waiter how much we had enjoyed ourselves.
b I still can't believe that she did so much for me. I will never, ever forget her.
c It was definitely the most exciting fairground ride I'd ever been on.
d At last we arrived home, tired but happy. I'll always remember the experience.
e The rain got worse and worse. In the end, we decided to go home.

2 Choose one of the titles from exercise 1 and write your own story. Write about 100 words.

13 TV and media

Vocabulary
The media

Write the answers using the words below.

programme	newspaper	magazine
journalist	documentary	commentator
radio	editor	presenter

a   two things you watch on TV ....
    ....

b   the person in charge of a newspaper ....

c   two things you can read ....

d   the person who tells you what's happening during a sports match ....

e   something you listen to but don't watch ....

f   someone who writes articles ....

g   the person who introduces a show ....

Reading   Part 5

Read the text about working on the radio. For each question choose the correct answer, A, B, C or D.

...On the radio...

Are you interested in working (1) .... the media? There are plenty of different jobs you can do, from assistant to presenter or DJ. We spoke to presenter Jake Jones to find out (2) .... he thought about his job on a local radio music station.

'When I was a child, I (3) .... to lie on my bed and listen to my favourite music station and dream of being a famous pop star. Unfortunately, I didn't use (4) .... very good at music and I couldn't sing, so there wasn't much hope for me. Then I thought about working in the media instead. When I left school, I (5) .... a course in journalism then I got a job as an assistant where I'm working now. I didn't use to (6) .... much money, but I did learn a lot about the radio station. I did all kinds of things such as organising paperwork, fetching packages and making coffee. After a couple of years I got promoted, and finally they asked me to (7) .... my own programme. It really is my perfect job and there's (8) .... I dislike about it.'

1   A on   B at   C in   D to
2   A which   B where   C why   D what
3   A used   B use   C using   D was used
4   A being   B to be   C to being   D be
5   A made   B had   C did   D gave
6   A earning   B earns   C earned   D earn
7   A present   B provide   C practise   D prepare
8   A everything B nothing   C something   D anything

Grammar
used to

1 Write the questions in an interview with a retired wildlife presenter. Use the prompts and *used to*.

a what / enjoy most / about the job?

....

b how often / travel abroad?

....

c which country / like / visiting most?

....

d which animal / feel / most afraid of?

....

e where / stay / during filming?

....

f how often / you / sleep / in the jungle?

....

2 For a–e complete the second sentence so that it means the same as the first. Use no more than three words.

a 100 years ago, nobody had a personal computer.
   People .... to have personal computers 100 years ago.

b I enjoyed watching cartoons as a child.
   When I was a child I .... enjoy watching cartoons.

c Before TV, people went to the cinema a lot.
   Before TV, people used .... to the cinema a lot.

d I hated flying five years ago.
   I didn't .... flying five years ago.

e At my old school, I didn't study hard.
   I .... to study hard at my old school.

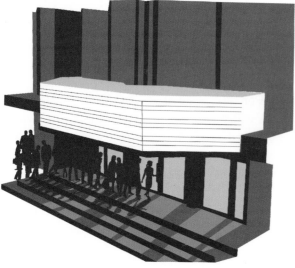

Vocabulary
TV programmes

Read the descriptions then write the missing letters to complete the words.

a A programme about animals is a
   w .... programme.

b A programme that's on several times a week and is about the same characters is a s ....
   o ....

c A presenter talks to famous people on a
   c .... show.

d An entertainment programme where you have to answer questions is a q .... show.

e A programme about real people in real situations is a r .... TV show.

f The programme that tells you about sun, rain, temperatures, etc. is the
   w .... forecast.

g A factual programme on a serious subject is called a d ....

Writing Part 2

1 Read the task and Luis' answer. What extra information has Luis included? Find and cross out three unnecessary sentences.

There is a documentary on TV tonight. Write an email to an English friend of yours. In your email, you should

➡ explain when the documentary is on

➡ describe what it is about

➡ say why your friend should watch it

Write 35–45 words.

Hi Mark

There's a fascinating documentary on TV tonight, which starts at 9 o'clock on Channel 3. There's also a good film on the other side, but I don't think you should watch that. The documentary's about modern graffiti artists in the US. I'm not very interested in art myself. I know how much you love street art, so I think you should watch it!

See you soon! Hopefully you'll be at Suzie's party!

Luis

2 Write your own answer to the task in exercise 1.

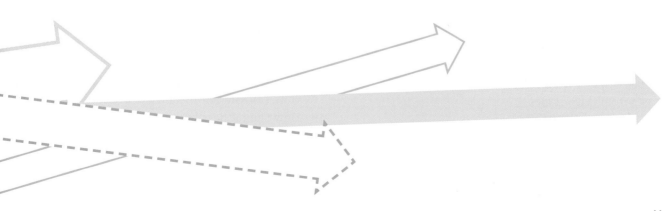

Reading Part 4

Using forensic psychologists to solve crimes has recently become very popular in TV shows. In these programmes, people use their knowledge of human behaviour to work out if people are telling the truth, and in real life, forensic psychologists are helpful in understanding criminal behaviour and helping police to solve crimes.

Being able to tell if someone is lying can be an important part of solving a crime. In the US they sometimes use a machine called a 'polygraph' or 'lie detector'. This is a machine which measures the heart rate, breathing and blood pressure while someone is answering questions. Any changes in the measurements may suggest whether this person is telling the truth or not. However, many experts believe that polygraphs are unreliable and often they are proved to be wrong. The police use other machines to help them decide if someone is lying. For example, they use computer software that examines what a suspect has written, a device that records voice changes, and even brain scans.

Some researchers believe that certain people have a special gift for spotting a liar. Dr Paul Ekman and Dr Maureen O'Sullivan from the University of California have researched this subject and believe that some people can tell from someone's voice and their expression if they are telling the truth.

So how can ordinary people like you and I tell if someone is lying? Look out for these signs: Are they hesitating more than usual? Are they sighing a lot, but using fewer hand gestures? Are their feet pointing towards an exit? Are they showing lots of nervous habits such as shrugging their shoulders? These are all pretty good signs that the person you are talking to may not in fact be telling the truth!

Read the text about lying. For questions 1–4 choose the correct answer A, B, C or D.

1 What is the writer's main purpose in writing the text?
   A to describe how bad it is to lie
   B to give advice about how to tell a lie
   C to discuss different ways of identifying lies
   D to explain why people tell lies

2 What would a reader learn about lie detector tests from this article?
   A They are all reliable.
   B They are only used in the US.
   C They all involve the use of machines.
   D They rely on physical changes in the speaker.

3 What does the writer say about Dr Paul Ekman and Dr Maureen O'Sullivan?
   A They think everyone can learn to detect lies.
   B They are both excellent at spotting liars.
   C They think it's impossible to be certain when someone is lying.
   D They believe some people are better at spotting lies than others.

4 Which of these is the best title for the article?
   A How can you tell if someone is lying?
   B How should liars be punished?
   C How often do people tell lies?
   D How many lies have you told?

Grammar

have something done

1 Use the prompts to write sentences saying what you can have done in places a–f.

bike / fix	car / wash
eyes / test	blood pressure / take
teeth / check	hair / cut

a   hairdresser's ....

....

b   optician's ....

....

c   doctor's surgery ....

....

d   dentist's ....

....

e   garage ....

....

f   bike shop ....

2 Rewrite each sentence a–f. Keep the same meaning and use the correct form of *have something done*.

a   A man is fixing their car at the moment.
They .... at the moment.

b   Somebody is testing my eyes tomorrow.
I .... tomorrow.

c   The hairdresser will style my mum's hair next week.
My mum .... next week.

d   They installed some new computers in our school yesterday.
We .... in our school yesterday.

e   The beautician is painting my sister's nails right now.
My sister .... right now.

f   Some men planted some trees in our neighbour's garden last year.
Our neighbours .... last year.

Listening   Part 3

▶7 You will hear part of a talk by a woman called Jessica, about changes in the way we communicate. For each question, fill in the missing information.

Changing communication

A talk by Jessica Fry

Topic:

How communication has changed in the last
(1) .... years.

The past:

We used to wait (2) .... for replies to letters and cards.
Young people communicated by writing (3) .... or phoning friends from home.
People used payphones instead of mobiles.

The present:

We can contact other people very (4) ....
Mobile phones help us stay in touch when away from home.

The disadvantages:

Apart from words, we communicate through

- the way we say something
- facial expressions
- our (5) ....

Vocabulary
Personal feelings

1 Match the feelings 1–8 with explanations a–h.

1 I'm really excited.
2 I'm feeling quite confident.
3 I'm so angry!
4 I'm feeling a bit embarrassed.
5 I'm so bored!
6 I'm a little bit frightened.
7 I feel lonely.
8 I'm very tired.

a I gave the wrong answer in front of everybody.
b I've just seen a horror film.
c I've had a lot of late nights recently.
d I've started at a new school and I don't know anyone.
e It's my birthday tomorrow!
f There's nothing to do!
g I think I passed the exam.
h My little brother broke my mobile phone.

2 Read the definitions then rearrange the letters to form the words. Check your answers in a dictionary.

a extremely pleased
  ghdedleit   d ....

b happy and smiling
  eeulhcrf   c ....

c feeling that something good is going to happen
  veopsiti   p ....

d a bit worried or afraid
  ounervs   n ....

e very unhappy
  seblmirae   m ....

f not worried or stressed
  erlxdae   r ....

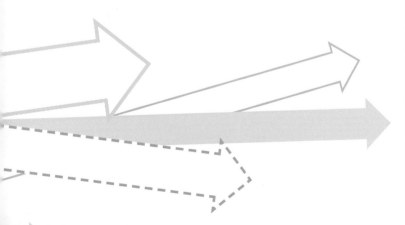

Writing   Part 3

1 Read the task and the story below. Complete 1–5 with a suitable adverb.

Your English teacher has asked you to write a story. Your story must have this title:

A silly mistake

Write your story in about 100 words.

I opened my eyes and (1) .... jumped out of bed. I had an important interview for a job to go to. In two minutes I was in the shower singing so (2) .... that my younger brother in the next room banged on the wall.

Twenty minutes later I was in the empty kitchen, wearing my best suit. 'The house is (3) .... quiet,' I thought, as I ate my breakfast (4) ....

Before long, I was at the bus stop. 'Where is everybody?' I wondered as I climbed onto an empty bus. Finally, I was outside the locked glass door of an office building and then I (5) .... realised. Today was Sunday, not Monday.

2 Write your own answer to the task in exercise 1. Use adverbs where appropriate.

Review 4 Units 11–14

1 Read the text below and for 1–10 choose the correct answer A, B, C or D.

The PizzaFest

It's September and I am at the World Pizza Festival in Naples, Italy. I've always loved Italian food. When I was a child, I (1)_____ to make pizza and other Italian dishes for my family, and now I work as a chef in an Italian restaurant in New York. In my opinion, nobody cooks as (2)_____ as the Italians, and many people think that the people in Naples make pizzas better (3)_____ anyone else in the world. So what happens at the festival? There is music and dancing and of course lots of pizza eating. You can (4)_____ your own favourite pizza created for you, or if you (5)_____ to, you can go to a workshop and learn how to make it yourself.

Yesterday, I (6)_____ a restaurant owner to explain the history of pizza. He (7)_____ me that the people of Naples made the first pizza. He (8)_____ that although flat bread is thousands of years old, people didn't use (9)_____ put ingredients on bread until the 19th century. Eventually, somebody made a topping that consisted (10)_____ tomatoes, mozzarella cheese and basil, ingredients with the colours of the Italian flag, and called it 'Margherita', after the Queen of Italy.

1	A use	B used	C to use	D using
2	A good	B better	C best	D well
3	A than	B as	C for	D of
4	A make	B do	C have	D take
5	A will want	B wanted	C want	D had wanted
6	A asked	B said	C told	D had
7	A said	B spoke	C asked	D told
8	A spoke	B said	C told	D asked
9	A to	B for	C with	D as
10	A of	B on	C from	D for

2 Complete the second sentence so that it means the same as the first. Use no more than three words.

a My sister is the best piano player in the family.
My sister plays the piano _____ anyone else in the family.

b I speak French worse than you.
I don't speak French as _____ you.

c 'Turn off your phone!'
The teacher told the student _____ his phone.

d 'Would you like a cup of coffee?'
She asked me _____ like a cup of coffee.

e 'Where are you going?'
My mum asked _____ was going.

f Ten years ago my dad worked in a bank.
My dad _____ work in a bank.

g If you plant seeds, they grow.
Seeds _____ you plant them.

h Somebody is fixing my laptop at the moment.
I _____ my laptop fixed at the moment.

3 For a–h decide which is the odd word out in each group and explain why.

a grapes   peas   onions   carrots
b email   text message   postcard   address
c packet   recipe   slice   spoonful
d sour   salty   snack   spicy
e comedian   commentator   editor   programme
f chat show   documentary   journalist   weather forecast
g excited   angry   embarrassed   bored
h delighted   cheerful   nervous   relaxed

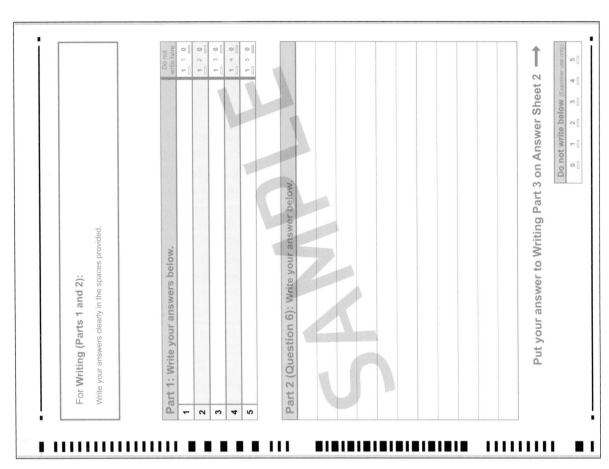

For **Writing** (Parts 1 and 2):

Write your answers clearly in the spaces provided.

Part 1: Write your answers below.

1

2

3

4

5

Part 2 (Question 6): Write your answer below.

Do not
write here

1 1 0
1 2 0
1 3 0
1 4 0
1 5 0

Put your answer to Writing Part 3 on Answer Sheet 2 →

Do not write below (Examiner use only)

0 1 2 3 4 5

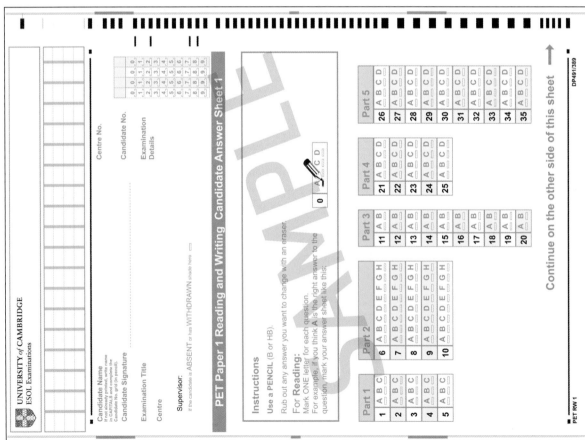

UNIVERSITY of CAMBRIDGE
ESOL Examinations

Candidate Name
If not already printed, write name
in CAPITALS and complete the
Candidate No. grid (in pencil).

Candidate Signature

Examination Title

Centre

Centre No.

Candidate No.

Examination
Details

Supervisor:
If the candidate is ABSENT or has WITHDRAWN shade here ▭

PET Paper 1 Reading and Writing   Candidate Answer Sheet 1

Instructions

Use a PENCIL (B or HB).

Rub out any answer you want to change with an eraser.

For Reading:
Mark ONE letter for each question.

For example, if you think **A** is the right answer to the question, mark your answer sheet like this:

0   A̲ B C D

Part 1

1 A B C
2 A B C
3 A B C
4 A B C
5 A B C

Part 2

6   A B C D E F G H
7   A B C D E F G H
8   A B C D E F G H
9   A B C D E F G H
10 A B C D E F G H

Part 3

11 A B
12 A B
13 A B
14 A B
15 A B
16 A B
17 A B
18 A B
19 A B
20 A B

Part 4

21 A B C D
22 A B C D
23 A B C D
24 A B C D
25 A B C D

Part 5

26 A B C D
27 A B C D
28 A B C D
29 A B C D
30 A B C D
31 A B C D
32 A B C D
33 A B C D
34 A B C D
35 A B C D

Continue on the other side of this sheet →

DP491/389

PET RW 1

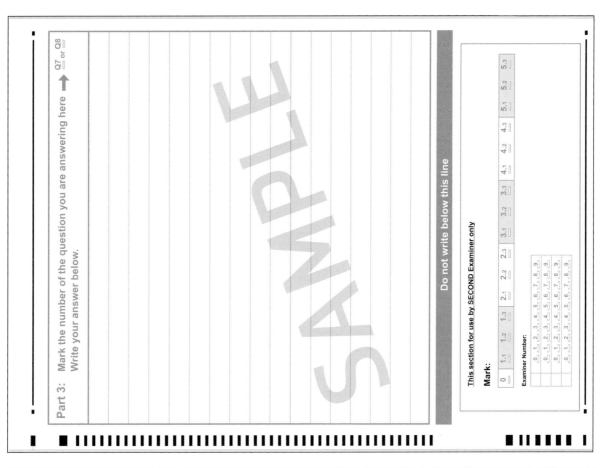

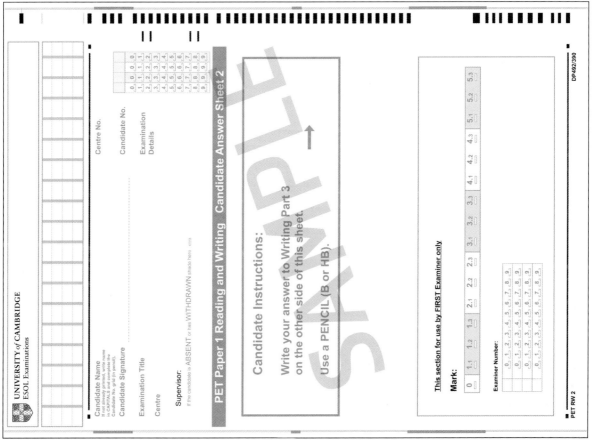

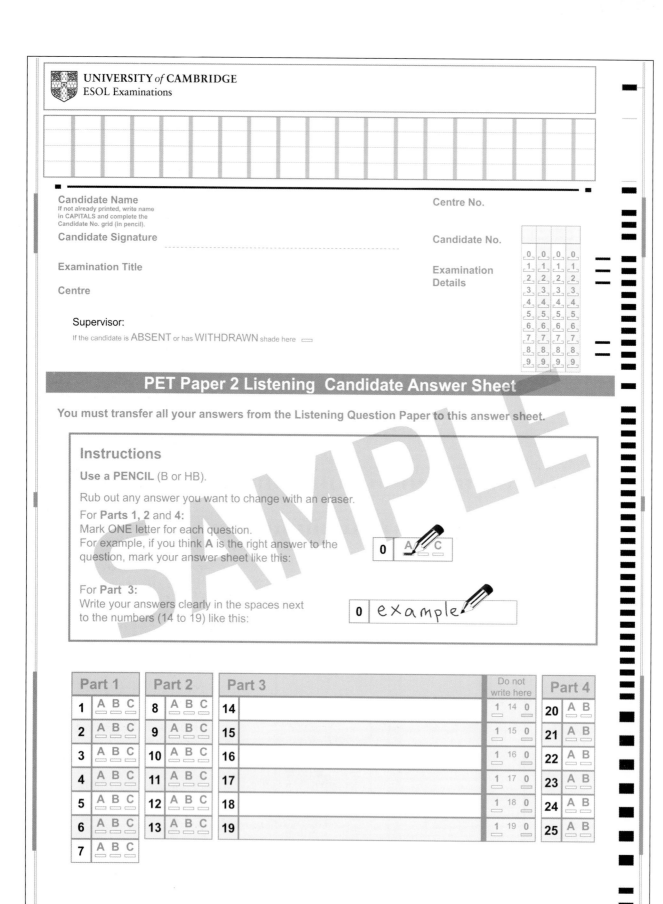

UNIVERSITY *of* CAMBRIDGE
ESOL Examinations

Candidate Name
If not already printed, write name
in CAPITALS and complete the
Candidate No. grid (in pencil).

Candidate Signature

Examination Title

Centre

Supervisor:
If the candidate is ABSENT or has WITHDRAWN shade here ▭

Centre No.

Candidate No.

Examination Details

PET Paper 2 Listening Candidate Answer Sheet

You must transfer all your answers from the Listening Question Paper to this answer sheet.

Instructions

Use a PENCIL (B or HB).

Rub out any answer you want to change with an eraser.

For **Parts 1, 2** and **4**:
Mark ONE letter for each question.
For example, if you think **A** is the right answer to the
question, mark your answer sheet like this:

For **Part 3**:
Write your answers clearly in the spaces next
to the numbers (14 to 19) like this:

Part 1	Part 2	Part 3	Do not write here	Part 4
1 A B C	8 A B C	14	1 14 0	20 A B
2 A B C	9 A B C	15	1 15 0	21 A B
3 A B C	10 A B C	16	1 16 0	22 A B
4 A B C	11 A B C	17	1 17 0	23 A B
5 A B C	12 A B C	18	1 18 0	24 A B
6 A B C	13 A B C	19	1 19 0	25 A B
7 A B C				

PET L

DP493/391

Key

Unit 1

Reading

1 correct
2 incorrect
3 incorrect
4 incorrect
5 incorrect
6 correct

Vocabulary

Transport

a helicopter, hot-air balloon
b elephant, horse, camel
c ferry, boat, ship, hovercraft
d motorbike, bicycle
e lorry
f underground train

Grammar

The past simple and past continuous

1 a I left the house at 8 o'clock this morning.
  b ✓
  c I was walking down the road when I met my neighbour.
  d My parents were waiting for me when my train arrived.
  e ✓
  f We were driving to France when the accident happened.

2 1 took
  2 didn't get
  3 explored
  4 went
  5 were
  6 were travelling
  7 made
  8 had
  9 were sailing
  10 taught

Vocabulary

At the airport

1 a passenger
  b boarding pass
  c terminal
  d customs
  e baggage
  f pilot
  g passport

2 a arrive
  b check in
  c collect
  d go
  e listen
  f wait
  g board

Grammar

Question words

a Where   e How
b Who   f Why
c How   g When
d What   h What

Articles

a –   g a
b The   h The
c an   i –
d –   j The
e The   k an
f –

Writing

1 Paragraph B does not belong.
The correct order is: D, C, A.

Unit 2

Reading

1 C
2 A
3 E

Grammar

Adverbs of frequency

a I am hardly ever late for school.
b We always study French on Fridays. / On Fridays we always study French.
c Our teacher usually gives us a test each week. / Usually our teacher gives us a test each week.
d My sister regularly studies until midnight. / My sister studies until midnight regularly.
e These children are often bored in class.
f I have never got 100% in an exam.

Listening

1 correct
2 correct
3 incorrect
4 incorrect
5 incorrect

▶ **Audioscript 1**

Joseph: We've got exams soon!

Sara: Yes, I know. Don't remind me.

Joseph: Have you done much revision?

Sara: Well, I've been studying every day for two weeks now.

Joseph: You've got nothing to worry about then! I only started last week.

Sara: Yes, but how many hours do you do every day?

Joseph: Four or five.

Sara: That's really good! I only do two.

Joseph: I think you should probably be doing more than that at this stage.

Sara: Yes, you're right I know, but I just find it so boring and I get so tired.

Joseph: You don't have to do all your revision at once. You could do a couple of hours in the morning and then do the rest later in the day. Some of my other friends do it that way. Personally, I prefer to do it all in the evenings, but that doesn't suit everyone.

Sara: Good idea. Anyway, this time next month, the exams will be over.

Joseph: Yeah and then we can celebrate. Shall we organise a party?

Sara: It's a good idea, but my flat's a bit too small for a party. I'm not sure my flatmates would agree to having it there.

Joseph: Well, we could have it at my place if you like. It's bigger and my flatmates won't mind.

Sara: All right then. So, when shall we have it?

Joseph: How about on Friday 25th?

Sara: But that's the very last day of the exams. I think the Saturday would be better – give us time to recover.

Joseph: But some people might go away then or have other plans. I think Friday's better.

Sara: Yes, you're probably right.

Joseph: We'll talk about food and music nearer the time – I have to go and revise now!

Vocabulary
make, do, have, take

1	B	4	C
2	C	5	B
3	A	6	A

Grammar
The present simple and present continuous
1 Are you thinking
2 offer
3 is starting
4 are
5 have
6 last
7 take
8 organise
9 go
10 are creating

Unit 3
Vocabulary
Shopping
1 a sales
b credit card
c discount
d receipt
e cost
f bargain
2 a pharmacy
b electrical store
c greengrocer's
d baker's / bakery
e music shop
f butcher's

Grammar
Countable and uncountable nouns

a	UC	f	UC
b	C	g	UC
c	C	h	UC
d	UC	i	C
e	C	j	C

Reading

1	A	3	B
2	B	4	C

Grammar
Quantity
Suggested answers
1 a some
b many
c any / some / a lot of
d How much
e ✓
f ✓
g any / many / some / lots of
h ✓
i How many

2
1	some	6	several
2	any	7	a few
3	little	8	a lot
4	a lot of	9	some
5	many		

Vocabulary
Clothes
1
1	jumper	8	sandal
2	skirt	9	trainer
3	necklace	10	belt
4	bracelet	11	T-shirt
5	boot	12	scarf
6	jeans	13	earring
7	trousers		

2
1	B	4	C
2	B	5	A
3	A		

Writing
1 Dear Marco
Thanks for your letter. It was great to hear from you. You asked me to tell you about my experience of learning English. Well, at the moment I'm doing an English course at a language school and I have lessons twice a week. We've got an American teacher and she's really nice.
Last summer I did a course at a language school in London. I really enjoyed being there and I met lots of really interesting people.
How are your family? Hope to hear from you soon.
Wen

Review 1
Units 1–3
1
1	B	6	A
2	D	7	C
3	A	8	B
4	D	9	D
5	B	10	C

2 a were travelling
b visited
c How
d the
e am never
f go
g have
h am thinking
i discount
j on
k do
l ever

3 a **ferry** The others are things you see in an airport.
b **hovercraft** The others cannot travel on water.
c **receipt** The others are kinds of shop.
d **belt** The others are kinds of footwear.
e **hat** The others are uncountable nouns.
f **elephant** This is the only animal.
g **scarf** The others are jewellery.
h **much** The others describe countable nouns.

Unit 4
Reading
1 A
2 D
3 C

Vocabulary
Parts of the body

a	wrist	e	stomach
b	eyes	f	legs
c	fingers	g	head
d	mouth	h	chest

Listening

1	B	4	A
2	B	5	A
3	C		

Welcome to *What's On* – the entertainment programme that tells you what's going on in your area. Let's start with the film festival that's on next Saturday and Sunday. You can buy weekend tickets in advance at the box office, or you can pay for each film individually. If you want to see two or more films though, paying for each film separately is expensive. There are no one-day tickets, I'm afraid.

The festival is organised by a local film club and its theme is 'animals in film'. There will be twelve films shown in total. I don't have a list of the final twelve at the moment and unfortunately the website is experiencing technical problems, but I'm expecting the information to be emailed to me any minute, so please stay with the programme.

One film they are definitely showing is the 1994 version of *The Jungle Book*. This isn't of course the original cartoon version – in this one Jason Scott Lee plays the part of the young boy that grew up with animals. He's still in the jungle with his animal friends, but now he's grown up and when an Englishwoman visits on safari, they fall in love. It's not a film that will please everyone, especially big fans of the original, but personally, I like the story just as much and the special effects are brilliant.

Try not to miss the 1986 version of *The Fly*, which has the same idea as the original made in 1958. Seth Brundle, played as you probably know by Jeff Goldblum, is a gifted but rather mad scientist, who is accidentally turned into a giant fly during an experiment. This is quite a scary horror film, so will be on later than the others.

One more film to mention is *Wolves: A Legend Returns to Yellowstone*. This is a documentary about the life of wolves in Yellowstone National Park in America. The film is narrated by Matthew Fox, and it features several important wolf experts and conservationists. The fantastic shots of the wolves are taken from helicopters as well as fixed cameras on the ground – these are unmanned, so they can get much better shots than a film crew at close range would be able to get. This is a wonderful film that I can't recommend highly enough.

Now let's move on to ...

Grammar
Comparative and superlative adjectives

a as intelligent
b better pets
c the fastest
d are as clever
e less cute
f easiest
g the most dangerous
h as important as

Vocabulary
Films

a	T	f	F
b	T	g	T
c	F	h	F
d	F	i	F
e	T	j	T

Unit 5
Vocabulary
Phrasal verbs

1
a give up
b get up
c throw away
d take up
e cut down on

2
a get up
b take up
c throw away
d cut down on
e gave up

Grammar
The imperative

a Don't eat unhealthy food.
b Don't smoke.
c Drink plenty of water.
d Wear good-quality trainers.
e Get to the gym early.
f Don't go to bed too late.

Reading

1	A	6	B
2	D	7	C
3	B	8	A
4	C	9	D
5	C	10	C

Grammar
The present perfect

1
a haven't ridden
b has started
c has become
d have finished
e hasn't seen
f has opened

2
1 **A:** Have you ever seen a crocodile?
   B: I have never seen a crocodile but I have held a snake.
2 **A:** Have you ever visited Thailand?
   B: I have never visited Thailand but I have travelled around India.
3 **A:** Have you ever flown in a helicopter?
   B: I have never flown in a helicopter but I have been in a hot-air balloon.
4 **A:** Have you ever climbed a mountain?
   B: I have never climbed a mountain, but I have crossed the Sahara Desert.

3
a for
b for
c since
d since
e for
f since

Vocabulary
Sport

a **baseball** The others are people involved in sport.
b **pitch** The others are sports equipment.
c **basket** The others are sports.
d **racket** The others are verbs.
e **goal** The others are places to do sports.
f **swimming** The others are not done in water / are played with a ball.

Writing

a haven't played
b won
c hasn't scored
d haven't played
e haven't been
f went
g hasn't passed
h has lived / has been

Unit 6

Listening

1 500 / five hundred / 5 hundred
2 one hour / 1 hour
3 floors
4 living room
5 July

▶ **Audioscript 3**

Good afternoon and welcome to Seattle Houseboat Tours. My name's Elizabeth Jones and I'm your guide today. This is my houseboat *Moonlight*. Before we go on board, I'd like to give you a little background information. Seattle has one of the largest numbers of houseboats in the US – about 500 of them in fact. That's quite a high number and shows how popular houseboat living is here. We're at the southern end of Lake Union right now and as you have probably seen already, this is a lively area with restaurants and shops and cafes. During our one-hour tour, you'll see a number of houseboats. People can pay millions of dollars for the biggest of these. Some of them are quite amazing and have two or three floors, which can include underwater cellars. My own is one of the smaller boats, but I still have plenty of room, as you'll see when I show you around. My living area includes one bedroom with an ensuite bathroom, plus a kitchen with plenty of cupboard space, and finally a living room. I also have electricity, running water and broadband Internet, so I really do have everything I need. You may be interested to know that I'm writing a book on the history of houseboats in the city, and this should be on sale from early July. Well, thank you for listening so far. Now let's move onto the boat and start the tour.

Grammar

The past perfect

1 1 e   4 b
   2 f   5 a
   3 d

2 a arrived / had already started
   b had never seen / went
   c had arranged
   d discovered / had lost
   e left / had ended
   f had got / closed

Reading

1 incorrect   5 correct
2 correct   6 incorrect
3 incorrect   7 correct
4 incorrect   8 incorrect

Vocabulary

Houses and homes

1 a kitchen
   b hall
   c city, village, countryside, town
   d balcony, patio
   e stairs
   f flat, bungalow
   g bathroom

2 a **curtain** The others are pieces of furniture.
   b **oven** The others are in the bathroom.
   c **fridge** The others are parts of a house.
   d **cupboard** This is the only piece of furniture.
   e **cottage** The others are rooms in a house.

Suffixes

a imaginative
b beautiful
c boring
d comfortable
e interesting
f wonderful

Negative prefixes

1 a inexpensive
   b unpleasant
   c unnecessary
   d inconvenient
   e impossible
   f incorrect
   g imperfect
   h unfashionable

2 a unfashionable
   b expensive
   c inconvenient
   d unpleasant
   e incorrect
   f impossible

Review 2
Units 4–6

1 1 C   6 D
   2 C   7 B
   3 A   8 A
   4 B   9 B
   5 C   10 C

2 a haven't seen
   b have / 've never been
   c have / 've been
   d had gone
   e the tallest
   f is better than
   g older than he
   h had seen

3 a house
   b yet
   c goalkeeper
   d countryside
   e curtains
   f balcony
   g tennis
   h scary

Unit 7

Reading

1 A   3 B
2 A   4 B

Vocabulary

Materials

a glass   e plastic
b wool   f metal
c cotton   g wood
d paper   h leather

Grammar

Order of adjectives

1

	Opinion	Size	Age	Shape	Colour	Nationality	Material
a	lovely	tiny					glass
b	incredible		old				china
c				circular	brown		wooden
d					white	Italian	leather
e		long		rectangular			metal
f	amazing		ancient			Egyptian	

2 a ✓
   b Anna's wearing a beautiful black silk dress.
   c I bought a tiny purple glass figure of a cat for my mother's birthday.
   d We saw a very interesting modern Russian version of *Romeo and Juliet*.
   e ✓
   f I went to a fascinating 12th century castle at the weekend.

Vocabulary

Entertainment

a stage
b scene
c entrance
d play
e audience
f costume

Grammar
Gerunds and infinitives

1 a to go
   b being
   c playing
   d to finish
   e meeting
   f to wait
   g to study
   h becoming
2 a before going
   b after eating
   c of getting
   d about playing
   e in joining

Writing

1 Isabella's letter doesn't say what her favourite part of the film is.

Unit 8

Reading

1 A   3 A
2 C   4 C

Grammar
Obligation, prohibition and necessity

Suggested answers
   a You need to know your way around the city very well.
   b You don't have to / don't need to be a sociable person, but it helps!
   c You must be / need to be a safe driver.
   d You must have a driving licence.
   e You mustn't drive if you're not feeling well.
   f You don't have to / needn't / don't need to / own your own cab, you can work for a company.
   g You mustn't drive over the speed limit.
   h You don't need satellite navigation but it could be useful.

Vocabulary
Household objects

1 a 5 corkscrew   f 2 frying pan
   b 1 fan   g 10 bucket
   c 8 tea-towel   h 7 mug
   d 3 iron   i 9 vase
   e 6 dustbin   j 4 lamp
2 a spoon   d plastic
   b saucepan   e cup
   c glass   f metal

Grammar
Ability and possibility

   a might   P
   b Can   A
   c can't   A
   d could   P
   e can't   A
   f may   P
   g might   P
   h can't   A

Listening

1 B   4 B
2 C   5 C
3 B

▶ Audioscript 4

1 **What will the weather be like later today?**
... and now on to today's weather. Well, it's been a cloudy start to the day with light winds in most places this morning. Heavy thunderstorms are expected to develop during the course of the day, so you can expect some fairly heavy rain and much stronger winds this evening. These should die out overnight, leading to a much quieter day tomorrow with the chance of sunshine.

2 **Who called the emergency services?**
... two schoolboys have been rescued from a cave after one of them fell and broke his wrist. The boys tried to use their mobile phones to call for help, but unfortunately there was no signal. Eventually they were found by other climbers who contacted the emergency services. Air-sea rescue returned with a helicopter and took the boys to safety. The parents say both boys are fine.

3 **How did the fire start?**
A: I heard there was a fire at your house earlier. Are you OK? Did your chip pan catch fire again?
B: No, it wasn't that this time. I was cooking chips in fact, but they were in the oven. No, this was an electrical fault – it turns out our old kettle was faulty and it burst into flames. I tried to put the fire out, but it spread too quickly, so I had to call the fire service.

4 **Where did the man leave the shopping?**
Woman: Goodness, I nearly tripped over those shopping bags. Why didn't you put them in the kitchen?
Man: Sorry. I was just coming

through the front door when the phone started ringing, so I put them down in the hall and rushed into the living room to answer the phone. It was Julie, by the way. She wants us to go round for lunch tomorrow.

5 **How did the woman find out about Anna's accident?**
Woman: Did you know that Anna is in hospital?
Man: Is she? I've just seen Paul and he didn't say anything about it.
Woman: He probably doesn't know yet. Anna only phoned me half an hour ago. Apparently, she slipped in a pool of water at work and fell down some stairs.
Man: How awful. I wouldn't be surprised if the story ends up in the local paper tomorrow. I do hope she's OK.

Vocabulary
The weather

   a T   e T
   b T   f F
   c F   g F
   d T   h F

Unit 9

Reading

1 incorrect   5 correct
2 incorrect   6 incorrect
3 correct   7 correct
4 incorrect   8 incorrect

Grammar
The passive

1   were made
2   own
3   are replaced
4   is estimated
5   aren't used
6   are left
7   are thrown
8   send
9   were used
10 were also given

Vocabulary
Technology

1 a keyboard   d laptop
   b software   e calculator
   c mouse   f screen
2 a hang up   d click
   b delete   e connect
   c dial   f enter

Grammar

Agreeing and disagreeing

1 So do I, So do I
2 Neither do I, So do I
3 So would I, so am I
4 Neither am I, So do I

Vocabulary

Work and jobs

1
a lorry driver
b dancer, actor, comedian
c waiter
d designer
e photographer, artist
f writer

2
a politician   e scientist
b librarian   f instructor
c director   g sailor
d producer   h musician

Writing

a are sold
b are grown
c was invented
d is watched by
e were stolen

Unit 10

Vocabulary

Personality adjectives

1 g	5 e
2 d	6 c
3 a	7 f
4 h	8 b

Phrasal verbs with *get*

1 d	5 a
2 b	6 c
3 f	7 e
4 g	8 h

Listening

1 incorrect	4 correct
2 incorrect	5 correct
3 incorrect	

▶ Audioscript 5

Jess: Hi, Billy. What are your plans for the weekend?

Billy: Well, I'm going to be quite busy. I'm going out with some people from work on Friday night.

Jess: Is somebody leaving? It's not you, is it?

Billy: Of course not! I've only just started! Quite a few people started with me and we thought it would be a good way to get to know each other if we went for a night out.

Jess: Are you going for a meal then?

Billy: No, we're going to that new nightclub in town.

Jess: Really? I wouldn't go there if I were you. I've heard it's very expensive.

Billy: Hmm, I hope not.

Jess: What are you doing on Saturday?

Billy: I'm going over to my parents' house for a family meal. It's my parents' anniversary.

Jess: That sounds like fun.

Billy: Yeah, it should be OK. I haven't seen my sister for a few months – she's away at university – so hopefully we can meet without arguing.

Jess: Do you usually argue then?

Billy: Quite a lot – usually about who should do the washing-up! The thing is, we're staying the night so we're going to have a lot of time together.

Jess: Maybe you should come home on Saturday night then.

Billy: I don't think there's much chance of that.

Jess: I was hoping you'd come with me to see a film on Sunday.

Billy: I doubt I'll have time. But I can give you a ring when I leave my parents' house.

Jess: Don't worry. Maybe we can go next week instead. Are you free on Friday?

Billy: Yes, I think so.

Reading

1
1 mine, it
2 The / My, It, you
3 you, Their / The
4 his, those / them, your / the

2
| 1 B | 3 C |
| 2 B | 4 C |

Grammar

The future

1
a I'm going to meet
b is going to be
c leaves
d I'll carry
e I'll be
f I'll come

2
1 e	4 d
2 a	5 b
3 c	6 f

3
1 am going to visit / am visiting
2 are going
3 are meeting / are going to meet
4 will probably be
5 starts
6 will pay

Review 3
Units 7–10

1
1 A	6 D
2 C	7 B
3 B	8 B
4 A	9 D
5 D	10 C

2
a are found
b was invented
c So
d Neither
e I'm meeting
f I'll eat
g leaves
h don't have to
i can't
j must

3
a T	e F
b F	f T
c F	g T
d T	h F

Unit 11

Reading

1 E
2 B
3 A

Vocabulary

Prepositions

1 in	5 ✓
2 of	6 on
3 on	7 ✓
4 in	8 about

Grammar

Zero and first conditional

a will rise   e won't be
b turn   f look
c won't have   g put
d don't stop   h want

Second conditional

a If my sister <u>had</u> a degree, she'd love to work in animal conservation.
b My parents wouldn't drive a car if public transport <u>were</u> / <u>was</u> more reliable.
c If I <u>were</u> / <u>was</u> very rich, I'd plant a forest of trees.
d I <u>wouldn't</u> ride a motorbike if I were you.
e If I <u>climbed</u> a mountain, I wouldn't leave any rubbish there.
f People would respect the environment more if they <u>were</u> fined for damaging it.

Vocabulary
Phrasal verbs

1
a up   d off
b out   e on
c up   f up

2 1 f   4 d
2 c   5 b
3 a   6 e

Writing

1 C

2 A I've met, interesting, Let's
B different, I'm meeting, Hope
C here, September, some time?

Unit 12
Vocabulary
Food

1
a milk, cheese, butter
b nut, fish, chicken
c carrot, pea, onion
d banana, apple, grape

2
a **steak** The others are methods of cooking.
b **honey** The others are fruits.
c **cereal** The others are vegetables.
d **tuna** The others are meat.
e **mushroom** The others are all flavourings for food.
f **jam** The others are salad vegetables.
g **slice** The others are for cooking and eating with.
h **toast** The others are used to eat with.

Grammar
Comparative and superlative adverbs

a My brother cooks better than anyone else in our house.
b ✓
c ✓
d I dress more smartly than usual when I go to a wedding.
e I play basketball as well as my friends. In fact, I'm probably better.
f ✓
g I worked the hardest in our class this year.
h ✓

Reading

1 correct   4 incorrect
2 correct   5 correct
3 incorrect   6 incorrect

Listening

1 1 C   4 B
2 C   5 A
3 B

▶ **Audioscript 6**

Presenter: Hello and welcome to *A Question of Taste*. On today's programme, I'm talking to food critic Josie Shepherd, who's going to tell us about her career. Welcome to the programme, Josie.

Josie: Thank you. It's a pleasure to be here.

Presenter: Being a food critic sounds like a fantastic thing to do. How did you become one?

Josie: Well, I've always had an interest in food. As a child, I was always in the kitchen, helping my parents with the cooking. In fact, neither of them was very keen on cooking, so they made recipes that were quick and uncomplicated, like roast meat and vegetables. I preferred experimenting with different spices and ingredients from around the world to try to create new tastes.

Presenter: So did you know from an early age that you wanted to be a chef?

Josie: I suppose I did. After I left school, I went to college and did a catering course. I enjoyed every aspect of it – the theory and the practical sides – and when I passed my exams, my tutors gave me excellent references so I was lucky enough to go straight to a restaurant in London, where I worked with a top chef.

Presenter: And how long were you there?

Josie: I was there for a year, but during that time, I realised that actually I didn't want a career as a chef. I found the pace of the work too fast and too stressful. There was never time to really think about or appreciate what I was doing. Don't get me wrong, the chefs there were incredibly talented and I learnt so much about how food works and how ingredients go together, which is of course very important for my job.

Presenter: So then you applied to do a course in journalism?

Josie: That's right. I did a course at a London college. I met some really interesting people, including the editor of a food magazine. When she found out about my background, she asked me to write an article on healthy eating – this was before I had even finished my course. Then she asked me to write a review of a fantastic restaurant called *Veggie*.

Presenter: Well, you clearly enjoy your work, Josie. Do you plan to carry on working as a food critic in the future, or would you like to go back to creating your own food?

Josie: I still cook at home and have dinner parties for my friends, so I don't miss that side of things. A friend of mine recently suggested buying a restaurant together, but I'm not too keen on that idea. What I'd really like is to start my own food magazine, maybe in about a year. In the meantime, I'll continue as I am, enjoying food and writing about it.

Presenter: Thank you very much, Josie. That was very interesting.

Grammar
Reported speech

1
1 Sam's mum asked him what he had eaten at school.
Sam told his mum that he had eaten a sandwich.
2 Liz asked Tom if he was hungry.
Tom said he was and asked Liz if she wanted to go to the cafe.
3 Anna told David not to touch her phone.
David said that he was sorry and that he didn't know that it was hers.
4 Mick asked Jessica what her favourite food was.
Jessica told Mick that she liked everything.
5 Millie asked her dad to tell her a story.
Dad asked Millie if she wanted a fairy tale.

2
a said   e said
b told   f told
c asked   g asked
d told   h said

Vocabulary
Tastes

a salty   e sweet
b bitter   f hot
c fishy   g spicy
d sour

Writing

1 1 b   3 a
2 e   4 d

Unit 13

Vocabulary
The media
a programme, documentary
b editor
c newspaper, magazine
d commentator
e radio
f journalist
g presenter

Reading
1	C	5	C
2	D	6	D
3	A	7	A
4	B	8	B

Grammar
used to
1
a What did you use to enjoy most about the job?
b How often did you use to travel abroad?
c Which country did you use to like visiting (the) most?
d Which animal did you use to feel most afraid of?
e Where did you use to stay during filming?
f How often did you use to sleep in the jungle?

2
a	didn't use	d	use to like
b	used to	e	didn't use
c	to go		

Vocabulary
TV programmes
a	wildlife	e	reality
b	soap opera	f	weather
c	chat	g	documentary
d	quiz		

Writing
1 Hi Mark
There's a fascinating documentary on TV tonight, which starts at 9 o'clock on Channel 3. ~~There's also a good film on the other side, but I don't think you should watch that.~~ The documentary's about modern graffiti artists in the US. ~~I'm not very interested in art myself.~~ I know how much you love street art so I think you should watch it!
See you soon! ~~Hopefully you'll be at Suzie's party!~~
Luis

Unit 14

Reading
1	C	3	D
2	C	4	A

Grammar
have something done
1
a You can have your hair cut.
b You can have your eyes tested.
c You can have your blood pressure taken.
d You can have your teeth checked.
e You can have your car washed.
f You can have your bike fixed.

2
a are having their car fixed
b am having my eyes tested
c will have her hair styled
d had some new computers installed
e is having her nails painted
f had some trees planted in their garden

Listening
1 30 / thirty
2 weeks
3 notes
4 quickly
5 body language

▶ Audioscript 7
Hello, my name's Jessica Fry. I'm here to talk about the importance of communication. We could go back thousands of years to look at the history of communication, but today I'd like to go back just thirty years, to when I was growing up in fact.
In those days, when we wanted to keep in touch with friends and relatives, we sent letters and cards through the post and often had to wait weeks for a reply. At school, we used to write notes to our friends, and in the evenings, we phoned them from our parents' landline – there were no mobile phones when I was a teenager! So, if we were out and needed to contact our parents, we had to use a public payphone. Of course, things are very different nowadays.
One of the main reasons for the way communication has changed is developments in technology. At home, we use email or instant messaging sites, and can contact several people at the same time. We can send messages and receive replies very quickly. When we're out and about we rely on our mobiles to keep in touch. For most of us this all seems very useful, but are there any disadvantages?

Well, there are a number of negative sides to this. First of all, communication is about more than just words. It's also about the way we say something. That includes things like the expression on our face, the way we stand, and our body language generally. Written messages can be misunderstood, especially if they're sent in a hurry with little thought given to spelling and punctuation.

Vocabulary
Personal feelings
1
1	e	5	f
2	g	6	b
3	h	7	d
4	a	8	c

2
a	delighted	d	nervous
b	cheerful	e	miserable
c	positive	f	relaxed

Writing
Suggested answers
1
1 quickly
2 loudly / badly
3 extremely
4 quickly
5 suddenly

Review 4
Units 11–14

1
1	B	6	A
2	D	7	D
3	A	8	B
4	C	9	A
5	C	10	A

2
a better than
b well as
c to turn off
d if I would
e me where I
f used to
g grow if
h am having

3
a **grapes** The others are vegetables.
b **address** The others are ways of communicating.
c **recipe** The others are quantities of food.
d **snack** The others describe how things taste.
e **programme** The others are people.
f **journalist** The others are kinds of TV or radio programme.
g **excited** The others are negative emotions.
h **nervous** The others are positive emotions.

oxfordenglishtesting.com

What is on the Workbook MultiROM?

The MultiROM in this Workbook Resource Pack has two parts.

- You can listen to the audio material that accompanies the workbook by playing the MultiROM in an audio CD player, or in a media player on your computer.

- You can also access two practice tests online with the MultiROM. Read the next page to find out about test features. To find out how to access them, read this page.

How do I use my MultiROM?

You will find your practice tests on a website called oxfordenglishtesting.com. The website contains many different practice tests, including the ones that you have access to. Because the practice tests are on the internet you will need:

- to be connected to the internet when you use the tests
- to have an email address (so that you can register).

When you're ready to try out your practice tests for the first time follow these steps:

1. Turn on your computer.
2. Connect to the internet. (If you have a broadband connection you will probably already be online.)

3. Put the MultiROM into the CD drive of your computer.
4. A screen will appear giving you two options. Single click to access your tests.

Single click here to access your practice tests

oxfordenglishtesting.com

Remember you must be online to access the website and your tests.

Workbook audio

You can play this CD in an audio CD player, or use the media player in your computer. If you want to listen to the audio on your computer use the media player.

What do I do when I get to the website?

After a few moments your internet browser will open and take you directly to the website and you will see this screen. Follow steps 1–3. If the screen does not appear follow step 4.

3 After filling in the registration form click on **Register**. To confirm your registration, click on **Save registration details**. Click on My tests where you will be asked to log in. You have one year to use the practice test before you have to submit it for final marking.

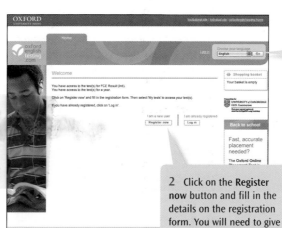

1 Choose a language from the drop-down list and click **Go**. All pages, apart from the actual practice tests, will be in the language you choose.

2 Click on the **Register now** button and fill in the details on the registration form. You will need to give an email address and make up a password. You will need your email address and password every time you log into the system.

4 The website knows which practice tests you have access to because it reads a code on your MultiROM. If the above page does not appear, go to www.oxfordenglishtesting.com/unlock You will be asked to click **Register now** if you are a new user. You will then be asked to fill in a registration form and to enter an unlock code. You can find the unlock code printed on your MultiROM. It will look like this 9219e6-9471d9-cf7c79-a5143b. Each code is unique.

Once you have registered, you can access your tests in future by going to oxfordenglishtesting.com and logging in. Remember you will need your email and password to log in. You must also be online to do your practice tests.

What are the features of each test?

Exam tips	You can see a tip on how to answer every question type.
Dictionary look-up	You can look up the meaning of any word in the practice test. Just double click it and a definition will pop up. You need to have pop-up windows enabled.
Instant marking and feedback	When you've answered a question, you can mark it straight away to see whether you got it right or wrong, and you can get feedback to find out why.
Change your answer or try again	You can then go back and have another go as many times as you like. Understanding why you answered a question incorrectly helps you think more clearly about a similar question next time.
Save and come back later	You don't have to complete a Paper in one go. When you log out it saves what you've done. You can come back to it at any time. You have 365 days before you have to submit the practice test for final marking. The **My tests** page tells you when the test expires.
Mark individual answers, a part, a paper or the whole test	However much you've done of the practice test, you can mark it and see how well you're doing.
Audio scripts	These are available for all parts of the Listening test. Reading the audio script will help you understand any areas you didn't understand when you were listening to them.
Sample answers for essay questions in the Writing paper	You can see *sample answers* after you've written your own. They've been written by real students, and will give you a good idea of what's expected. The essay you write will not be marked automatically. If you would like your teacher to mark it, you can print it off to give to them or email it to them. When they've marked it, you can enter the mark on your **Results** page. It does not matter if you do not enter a mark for the essay. The final marks will be adjusted to take that into account.
Useful phrases for the Speaking paper	You get sample Speaking papers and *Useful language* to help you practise offline. You can print the Speaking paper from the **Learning Resources** page, and ask your teacher to do the Speaking paper with you. As with the Writing paper, you can enter the mark your teacher gives you. However, even if you don't, your final marks will be adjusted to take that into account.
Results page	Remember this is a practice test not the real exam. You will see your score by paper and part and as a percentage. You will only get an indication as to whether your score is equivalent to a pass or not.
Try a sample test first	You can try out a short version of a practice test on oxfordenglishtesting.com before you do a real one. This lets you find out how to use a test before you start.
Buy more practice tests	To get even more practice you can buy more tests on oxfordenglishtesting.com